THE
Partytime
COOKBOOK

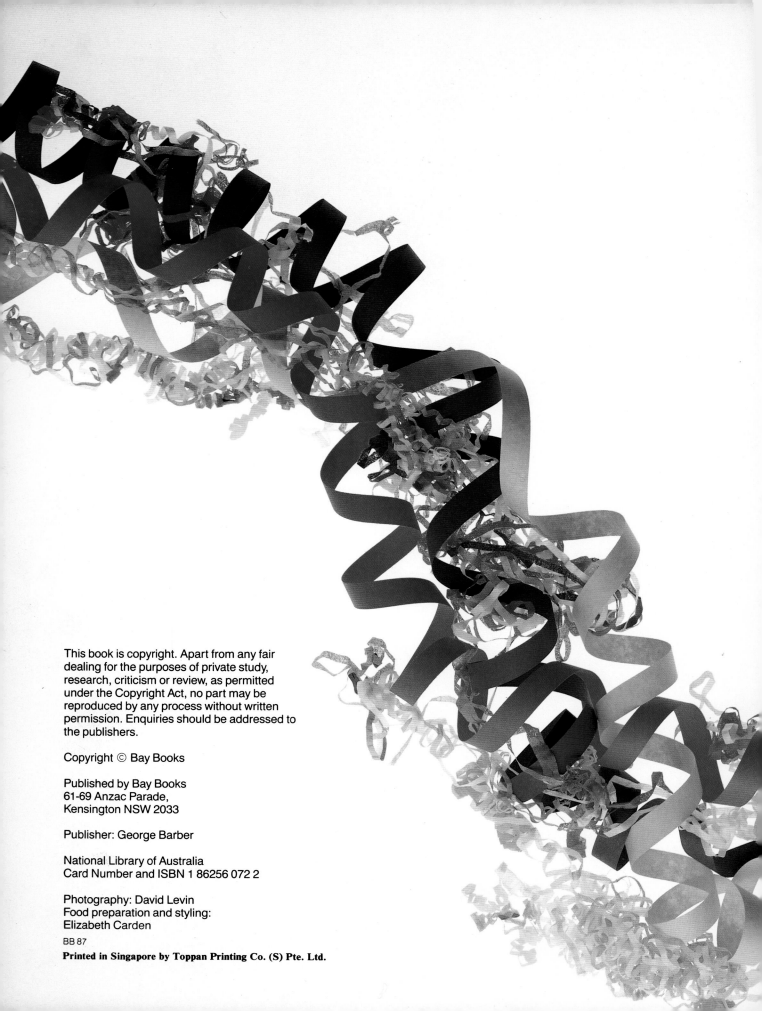

Copyright © Bay Books

Published by Bay Books
61-69 Anzac Parade,
Kensington NSW 2033

Publisher: George Barber

National Library of Australia
Card Number and ISBN 1 86256 072 2

Photography: David Levin
Food preparation and styling:
Elizabeth Carden

BB 87
Printed in Singapore by Toppan Printing Co. (S) Pte. Ltd.

THE
Partytime
COOKBOOK

JANE ASPINWALL

JAN WUNDERLICH

BAY BOOKS
Sydney and London

Contents

Let's Have a Party!

Any reason for a party is a good reason. Whether you're celebrating a very special affair such as a wedding or anniversary in grand style, or simply in the mood for sharing a good time with those you care about, having a party is one of the best ways to socialise and enjoy life.

The art of entertaining well depends on planning and experience. If you're a first time party giver, you'll probably feel a few doubts about your organisational abilities. Don't fret, simply opt for an easy party outdoors such as a picnic or a barbecue, which involve a minimum of fuss and bother. Each time you entertain you'll gain more confidence until you can branch out into something more complicated. For the experienced host, you might like more of a challenge, such as a fancy cocktail party or a formal dinner dance.

WHAT SORT OF PARTY CAN YOU AFFORD?
As with most things in life, the type and size of your party usually depends on your finances. When you set down your party budget, list all the expensive items such as food, drink, decorations and flowers, invitations, equipment rentals (chairs, glassware, cutlery, lighting, etc.) and proceed to eliminate those you can. If your mother, sister or next door neighbour has a particularly splendid garden full of blooms, they may let you select a few for decorative purposes, and you'll probably be able to borrow extra seating from friends and family.

Drawing up a guest list to suit your budget can be difficult. How do you possibly *not* invite one couple when you've decided to invite others? This is always a personal dilemma but if you're tactful and graceful, you shouldn't harm too many friendships. Consider scaling down other areas of

expense in order to accommodate an extra guest or two . . . often, it's the only real solution.

THE RIGHT MIX OF PEOPLE
What makes some parties buzz with excitement and fun while others tend to fizz out in unfulfilled expectation? Mostly, it's the blend of people that determines the life of the party. Too many talkers and not enough listeners can result in a loud and obnoxious group who are continually fighting for centre stage, while a thoughtful bunch of philosophers will most likely spend the night mumbling into their beards! Mix interests, lifestyles and age groups till you have a marvellous medley from all walks of life — then watch the conversation crackle!

If you're an inexperienced host, do yourself a favour and avoid a large gathering; invite only those friends and family you feel comfortable with. If disaster does strike (and one day, dear reader, it will), at least with a team of friendly faces around you, you will be able to grin and bear it!

INVITATIONS
An informal party calls for little more than a quick telephone call or a casual mention at your next encounter. More formal occasions — weddings, engagements and christenings for example, will always call for a letter or invitation card. You can make these yourself if you have the time and creativity; your guests will be pleased with your extra thoughtfulness and find it an invitation hard to refuse. Make sure you specify all the vital information: date, time, address, type of party, attire (formal, informal, fancy dress or 'come as you are'), telephone number, reply address and an RSVP date. If you're holding the party at an unusual venue that may be unfamiliar to the guests, it's always wise to include a map or directions. Try to

issue post and telephone invitations on the same day, so that no one will feel they're an afterthought. And if you do suddenly remember someone you had left off the list, don't try to make excuses; just issue a casual 'Are you free on such-and-such for a little get together I'm having?' Don't make a fuss and you'll be saved from embarrassment.

CHILDREN
Always be prepared for entertaining children. They usually don't want to be part of the adults' party so try to give them something amusing to do on their own. Videos and popcorn can be very useful.

If you have children of your own, ask friends to bring theirs along — this way you won't have to worry about your brood getting bored and your guests will save on babysitting costs.

Babies should be in a convenient bedroom away from the noise but near the parents, who'll probably spend all night ducking in and out to check on them.

NEIGHBOURS
People and parties inevitably mean noise — sometimes more noise than you had anticipated! Show your neighbours some consideration by observing noise pollution curfews if they apply in your neighbourhood. Ask rowdy guests to move inside the house where more noise can be absorbed; issue guests with parking suggestions if off-street sites are limited and make sure they don't encroach on your neighbours' private land. The best neighbour-taming method is to invite your immediate neighbours to join in — they may decline the invitation but appreciate it anyway.

CONSIDER A THEME
Consider special effects for both formal and casual occasions: you can go all the way and ask your guests to dress up appropriately, or simply use the theme as a way of linking food, music, lighting and venue. Possible themes might be Sixties, gangster, Australiana, any nationality, colour

(e.g. black and white), buffet, formal, beach, riverside picnic. If holding a fancy dress party, make sure you give your guests plenty of time to invent their costumes. Remember, a theme gives people something to focus on; it can make planning easier for you and the party much more unusual and exciting for your guests.

MENU PLANNING
There's no need to spend hours in the kitchen in order to provide spectacular party fare: all you need is the right mix of food and a little care in its presentation. Visualise the food and drink you intend to serve as a painting — look for balance and harmony in colour, taste and texture. Choose exciting and different ways to garnish plates and serving dishes as this can make all the difference to the 'eye appeal' of the food, no matter how tasty it is.

Your main guidelines for menu planning should be based around the occasion itself; what's good fare for one party may be inappropriate for another. Never experiment with new dishes on the day or night of the party — always stick with tried and true successes (but not the same dish over and over to the same guests, please!) or have a test run a week before. Combine interesting flavours and colours, and watch for too much soft or too much hard food served together.

PLAN AHEAD
Do try to make things easy for yourself by doing as much preparation ahead of time as possible. All-important mood setters like lighting and music, should be thought about well in advance, leaving no room for last minute panic. Decorations such as flowers can be arranged the day before. Easy-to-prepare-and-serve foods will leave the host more relaxed and able to enjoy the occasion just as much as the guests. Many dishes can be frozen successfully, leaving only garnishes to be added. The better the planning, the greater your enjoyment will be.

Children's Party Checklist

★ Choose a location, theme and time, the more original, the better.

★ Send out interesting invitations two to three weeks ahead; try to keep the guest list small.

★ Choose the menu and do as much as possible ahead of time. (Check now if any guests have special dietary needs.)

★ Prepare house for the intended horde — clear away all valuables and establish 'off limits' boundaries such as bedrooms, studies, etc.

★ Ensure that all children can be delivered and picked up at the nominated times; have a list of contact numbers for parents in case of emergency or illness.

★ Ask another adult to help out and give you support for the afternoon. You'll need it!

★ Decorate party area with balloons, streamers and posters, anything that's bright and cheery.

★ Give the children plenty of room to move and make a mess; preferably outdoors.

★ Have on hand a good supply of prizes, at least one for every child. Extras may come in handy in case of tantrums!

★ Be sure your home and yard are safe for party activities; inform your neighbours of the event so they can keep a lookout for 'escapees' and wanderers!

★ Keep pets away from the party zone; they may frighten timid guests or tempt little terrors!

★ Arrange a set of rainy-weather alternative games and activities.

★ Assemble goodie bags as far ahead of time as possible; make a few spares for last-minute arrivals and some for brothers and sisters.

Apple Bobbing: Best as an outdoor activity, fill large tubs or buckets with water, place whole or halved apples in the water and challenge children to retrieve the apples using teeth only. Sure to cause a few splashes but lots of fun!

Musical Statues: A variation on the musical chairs theme, each guest must dance and move about while the music is played; when it stops suddenly, each must freeze perfectly still. Those who fail to do so are eliminated until there's a final winner.

Treasure Hunt: With secret little treasures hidden throughout the house and garden, issue each guest a clue that leads them to the next clue, and the next, until eventually they uncover the booty. Small amounts of coin money are always well-received!

Eat The Chocolate: Watch how fast children consume the prize in this game! You'll need a hat, gloves, sunglasses, scarf and pair of large boots plus a jumbo-sized block of chocolate, knife, fork and plate. Place the above in the middle of a circle of children and give them a couple of dice. Each child takes turns at rolling the dice until someone lands on a six; they then leap into the middle of the circle, don all the apparel then begin to eat the chocolate using the knife and fork. Meanwhile, the other players continue to roll the dice until another six is thrown. The winner then assumes the chocolate-eating role, even if the previous winner has only just managed to fit the gloves! It's frenzied fun in a mad race for just one bite of the chocolate!

Special Celebrations

Fabulous food for those special occasions whether dressed up or a casual get together — anniversaries, birthdays to remember, engagements, weddings, christenings, victories or simply time to have a party. These recipes have been chosen to impress guests while being easy to prepare and serve for buffets, cocktail parties or even sit-down affairs.

Savoury Starters

GUACAMOLE

4 ripe avocados
juice 2 lemons *or* limes
1 teaspoon salt (optional)
2 large onions, grated
2 cloves garlic, crushed
2 teaspoons curry powder
pinch cayenne
few drops Tabasco sauce (optional)
chopped red chillies, to garnish
taco or corn chips, to serve

Mash avocados with fork or blend in food processor. Add lemon juice and salt. Add remaining ingredients to avocado. Cover with plastic wrap and chill to serve. Spoon into 2 bowls before serving. Garnish with chopped red chillies. Serve with taco chips and vegetable sticks.
Note: For this versatile Mexican dish it is good to look for over-ripe avocados. If preparing in advance mash avocados with a wooden spoon and store the finished guacamole in a jar with the avocado seeds. This will prevent discolouring.
Makes 4 cups

Raw Vegetables with Hot Dip and canapes

CHICKEN LIVER PATE

1 kg chicken livers
185 g butter
2 cloves garlic, crushed
4 tablespoons dry sherry
5 tablespoons brandy
1 tablespoon chopped parsley
½ teaspoon fresh thyme leaves
pinch cinnamon
pinch grated nutmeg
salt and freshly ground pepper, to
    taste
¼ cup thickened cream

Clean chicken livers. Heat 90 g butter, add garlic and cook for 30 seconds. Add chicken livers and cook for 5 minutes or until almost cooked. Puree chicken livers and cooking liquid in a bowl.
Heat remaining butter. Add remaining ingredients except cream and heat through. Pour over chicken livers and beat well. Stir in cream, taste and adjust seasoning. Spoon mixture into a serving container, cover and chill. Serve with crackers.
Serves 10–12

HOT DIP FOR RAW VEGETABLES

5 cloves garlic
2 tablespoons milk
1¼ cups olive oil
60 g butter
120 g anchovies, finely chopped

Chop garlic very finely and leave it in the milk for a few hours to take away some of its pungency. Put oil and butter in a heatproof earthenware pot, add anchovies and drained garlic and cook on very low heat for about 15 minutes, stirring from time to time. Serve immediately, with prepared vegetables.
Serves 4

COUNTRY COMBINATION PATE

1 onion, chopped
1 clove garlic, crushed
sprig thyme
sprig parsley
sprig chervil
60 g butter
250 g chicken livers, cleaned
salt and pepper, to taste
125 g fat pork, roughly chopped
125 g lean pork, roughly chopped
6 bacon rashers

Gently cook onion, garlic and herbs in butter for 1–2 minutes, then add livers diced into 2 cm pieces, and cook gently for about 1 minute. Cool, then season and puree with pork.

Line a terrine with rashers of bacon and spoon in meat mixture, covering it with more bacon rashers. Stand terrine in a baking dish half-full of water and bake at 180°C (360°F) for 1 hour. Cool, then refrigerate until firm. When chilled, slice pate and serve on lettuce leaves, accompanied by triangles of toast.
Serves 8

SMOKED FISH PATE

4 smoked mackerel fillets *or* 2 whole
    smoked mackerel
juice 2 limes *or* 1 lemon
125 g packet cream cheese, softened
200 g butter, melted
pepper, to taste
sprigs fresh herbs such as dill, fennel,
    flat-leaved parsley
lemon slices, to garnish
Melba toast or crackers, to serve

Skin and flake mackerel. Place in a blender or food processor with lime juice, cream cheese and butter. Blend to a puree. Season with pepper.

Turn into a suitable size serving dish and chill for several hours. Garnish with fresh herbs and lemon slices.

Serve with Melba toast or crackers.
Serves 4–6

TARAMASALATA

2 slices stale wholemeal bread
75 g smoked cod's roe
1 clove garlic, crushed
pinch cayenne pepper
juice 1–2 lemons
paprika, to taste
⅔ cup oil

Remove crusts from bread and soak slices in a little water. Remove skins from cod's roe and pound to a smooth paste. Squeeze bread dry and add to roe with garlic and cayenne pepper. Continue to pound mixture until it is really smooth. Gradually stir in lemon juice and oil and beat vigorously. Transfer to serving dish, sprinkle with paprika and serve with toast.
Note: All ingredients can be put in a blender or food processor and blended until smooth.
Serves 4

OYSTER CHEESE PUFFS

125 g butter
1½ cups grated tasty cheese
2 teaspoons sherry
1 egg, separated
2 x 105 g cans smoked oysters, drained
32 x 4 cm bread rounds
1 tablespoon finely chopped parsley
paprika, to taste

Beat butter, cheese and sherry together. Add egg yolk and blend well. Whisk egg white till soft peaks form. Fold egg white into cheese mixture.

Place 1 oyster on each round of bread. Top with a teaspoonful of cheese mixture. Sprinkle with chopped parsley and paprika. Place on oven trays. Bake at 230°C (450°F) for 10 minutes and serve piping hot.
Makes 32

CRUNCHY CHICKEN LIVERS WITH SOUR CREAM DIP

oil, for deep-frying
⅓ cup corn meal
¼ cup flour, sifted
½ teaspoon salt
½ teaspoon garlic salt
pinch pepper
1 egg
2 tablespoons milk
7 chicken livers, cleaned and cut into
    2 cm pieces
SOUR CREAM DIP
1 cup sour cream
2 tablespoons grated onion
½ teaspoon salt
¼ teaspoon Worcestershire sauce
1 teaspoon French mustard
4 drops Tabasco *or* chilli sauce

Combine all dip ingredients, cover and refrigerate until ready to serve.

Heat sufficient oil in a small, straight-sided pan to come half-way up the sides. Carefully heat oil while preparing chicken livers.

Combine corn meal, flour and seasoning. Mix egg with milk. Dip each piece of liver into seasoned corn meal, then into egg mixture and then into corn meal again.

Deep-fry at 190°C (375°F) for 2 minutes or until golden brown. Serve hot on toothpicks with dip.
Note: These appetisers can be prepared in advance. To reheat livers place in a 180°C (350°F) oven for about 10 minutes.
Makes about 30 appetisers and 1 cup dip

SMOKED SALMON QUICHE

PASTRY
2 cups flour
salt, to taste
125 g butter
3–4 tablespoons cold water
FILLING
185 g smoked salmon
4 egg yolks, beaten
4 whole eggs, beaten
300 mL sour cream
2 tablespoons lemon juice
¾ cup cream
½ teaspoon cayenne pepper
freshly ground pepper
½ cup grated Swiss cheese

Preheat oven to 200°C (400°F). Sift flour and salt into a bowl. Rub in butter to resemble breadcrumbs. Add sufficient water to form a soft dough. Knead lightly on floured board. Roll out dough to fit 20 cm flan tin. Prick base of case with fork. Bake pastry case for 10 minutes.

Layer salmon in pastry case. Blend egg yolks, eggs, sour cream, lemon juice, cream, cayenne and black pepper. Strain and pour into pie case. Top with grated cheese.

Bake at 190°C (375°F) for 45-60 minutes or until set and browned on top. Cut into slices and serve hot or cold.
Serves 12–16

Left to right: Country Combination Pate and Smoked Fish Pate

A selection of party canapes

CANAPES

Canapes provide a bite-sized starter to any party. Remove crusts from white, wholemeal or rye bread. Toast or pan-fry bread slices. Brown both sides. Cut bread slices into 2.5 cm squares, rounds or use a small scone or biscuit cutter to cut bread into shapes. Allow toasted bread shapes to cool.

Cheese pastry shapes can be made as an alternative to bread shapes. Make a quantity of cheese pastry, roll out thinly, cut into various shapes and bake. A variety of savoury crackers can also be used.

TASTY TOPPINGS

SPICY SARDINE
60 g butter
1½ teaspoons lemon juice
1½ teaspoons prepared mustard
sardines *and* pimiento, to garnish

Combine ingredients and spread toast or crackers with mixture. Top with ½ sardine and a thin strip pimiento.
Makes ⅓ cup

SMOKED OYSTER OR MUSSEL
1 quantity Spicy Sardine Topping *(see recipe)*
105 g can smoked oysters *or* mussels
finely chopped parsley, to garnish

Butter toast as for Spicy Sardine Canapes. Top each with smoked oyster or mussel. Sprinkle with finely chopped parsley.

CREAM CHEESE
250 g cream cheese, softened
105 g can drained, smoked oysters *or*
¼ cup finely chopped pecans *and*
pinch cayenne pepper *or*
¼ cup finely chopped chicken meat *and*
pinch dry mustard *and*
1 tablespoon chopped parsley
parsley, fresh herbs *or* watercress, to garnish

Combine ingredients, spread on toasts or crackers and garnish.
Makes approximately 1¼ cups

FILO DELIGHTS

375 g packet filo pastry
200 g butter, melted
SEAFOOD FILLING
¼ cup cottage cheese
220 g can crabmeat, drained
2 shallots, chopped
salt and pepper, to taste
SPINACH CHEESE FILLING
4 leaves spinach, shredded and cooked
1 small onion, chopped
30 g feta cheese, crumbled
½ teaspoon lemon juice
pepper, to taste
CHILLI MEAT FILLING
125 g cooked mince meat
1 tablespoon chilli sauce or to taste
1 small onion, chopped
CREAM CHEESE FILLING
125 g cream cheese, softened
2 shallots, chopped
salt and pepper, to taste

To prepare the fillings, combine ingredients adjusting seasoning as necessary.

Place pastry between 2 dry tea towels and cover with a just damp tea towel. Take 2 sheets of pastry and place 1 on top of the other. Cut pastry into 6 pieces, across the width. Brush each piece of pastry with a little butter.

Place a teaspoonful of selected filling in left-hand corner of pastry. Fold other corner of pastry up to cover filling to form a triangle shape. Fold left-hand corner up to form second triangle. Continue folding in triangles to the end of the pastry. Brush with melted butter. Repeat with remaining pastry and fillings.

Place on baking tray. Bake at 200°C (400°F) for 15–20 minutes until golden brown. Serve hot.
Note: Filo Delights can be filled in advance. Layer uncooked triangles between sheets of plastic wrap and freeze for up to 2 weeks. Place frozen into hot oven to cook and brown.
Makes approximately 50

PRAWN AND CHEESE PASTRIES

PASTRY
1½ cups flour
pinch salt
100 g butter
½ cup grated cheese
2 tablespoons cold water
FILLING
½ cup chopped cooked prawns
1 cup grated tasty cheese
1 tablespoon chopped leek
4 eggs
½ cup cream
½ cup milk
pinch mustard powder
grated rind 1 lemon
salt and pepper, to taste

Preheat oven to 190°C (375°F). Sift flour and salt into a bowl. Rub in butter to resemble breadcrumbs. Mix in cheese and sufficient water to form a soft dough. Knead lightly on floured board. Roll out thinly and cut into 24 x 6 cm rounds to fit patty tins.

Press pastry gently into base of tins. Place small amount of chopped prawns into base of pastry. Top with portion each of cheese and leek. Blend together eggs, cream, milk, mustard, lemon rind, salt and pepper. Spoon egg mixture over prawns and cheese.

Bake pies at 190°C (375°F) for 15–20 minutes or until golden and puffy. Serve hot or cold.
Makes 24

Left to right: Filo Delights and Prawn and Cheese Pastries

HAM AND MUSHROOM PASTRIES

4 sheets frozen ready-rolled puff
    pastry, thawed
1 egg, beaten
FILLING
125 g ham, diced
1 onion, chopped
125 g mushrooms, sliced
30 g butter
1 stick celery, chopped
1 tablespoon chopped parsley
2 teaspoons tomato puree or paste
pepper, to taste

Fry ham, onion and mushrooms in butter until onion is transparent. Add celery, parsley, tomato puree and pepper. Heat until liquid has evaporated. Remove from heat and cool.

Cut pastry sheets into 9 rounds, using a 10 cm cutter. Place a tablespoonful of mixture on one half of each round. Fold over pastry to form half moon shape. Press edges together to seal, and use prongs of a fork for decoration. Brush with beaten egg.

Place pastries on baking tray. Bake at 220°C (420°F) for 15–20 minutes. Serve hot or cold.
Makes 36

SMOKED FISH CREAMS

275 g smoked haddock fillets
salt and freshly ground pepper, to
    taste
freshly grated nutmeg, to taste
2 eggs, beaten
275 mL thickened cream
sprigs fresh dill, to garnish

Carefully skin fish and cut into pieces. Place in an electric blender with herbs and process to a smooth puree. Blend in eggs and transfer mixture to a bowl. Cover and refrigerate overnight.

Preheat oven to 290°C (375°F). Fill a large roasting pan with about 2.5 cm boiling water and place in centre of oven. Return fish mixture to blender with cream and blend thoroughly. Lightly grease 8 x 6 cm ramekin dishes and fill them three-quarters full with mixture. Place ramekins in roasting pan and bake for 30 minutes.
Serve creams immediately, either in ramekins or turned out onto plates. Garnish with fresh dill.
Serves 8

The Main Meal

CREAMY CRAYFISH CURRY

80 g butter
1 small onion, finely chopped
1 green apple, peeled, cored and
    chopped
12 peppercorns
⅓ cup flour
2½ teaspoons curry powder
1 bay leaf
pinch nutmeg
2½ cups milk
2 teaspoons lemon juice
½ teaspoon Worcestershire sauce
extra 60 g butter
750 g uncooked crayfish meat,
    chopped
¼ cup cream
2 tablespoons sherry
1 tablespoon finely chopped parsley, to
    garnish
OPTIONAL ADDITIONS
20 g butter
1 cup diced carrot
1 cup frozen peas
1 red or green capsicum, diced
90 g button mushrooms

In a saucepan, heat butter and saute onion, apple and peppercorns over medium heat until onion is transparent. Add flour, curry powder, bay leaf, and nutmeg and cook for 1 minute. Stir in milk, lemon juice and Worcestershire sauce. Bring slowly to boil and simmer until mixture thickens, stirring continually. Cook 1–2 minutes longer, taste and adjust seasoning.

Strain sauce through a fine sieve, pressing vegetables against sieve to extract all sauce.

Melt extra butter in frying pan. Saute lobster meat for 3 minutes. Remove from heat and set aside. Saute any optional additions and combine with curry sauce, cream and sherry. Gently heat through and fold in lobster meat. Simmer for 2 minutes. Spoon curry into serving dish. Sprinkle with chopped parsley.
Serves 6

CURRY VARIATIONS

CURRY OF PRAWNS
Replace crayfish meat with
500g shelled uncooked prawns
Serves 6

CURRY OF CHICKEN
Replace crayfish meat with
750 g diced chicken meat or
1.5 kg chicken pieces
Serves 6

PARTY CRAB CREPES

16-18 crepes (see recipe)
FILLING
20 g butter
6 mushrooms, sliced
2 tablespoons finely chopped onion
225 g crabmeat, drained
20 g extra butter
⅓ cup flour
½ teaspoon rosemary
salt and pepper, to taste
1½ cups chicken stock
1½ cups sour cream
1 tablespoon chopped parsley
1 cup grated Swiss cheese
paprika, to taste
parsley, to garnish

To prepare filling, melt butter in frying pan. Add mushrooms and onion and saute 3 minutes. Add crabmeat, remove pan from heat.

Melt extra butter in another saucepan. Add flour, rosemary, salt and pepper and cook, stirring constantly, for 3 minutes. Gradually stir in chicken stock, bring to boil and cook for 3 minutes. Add sour cream, parsley and ½ cup Swiss cheese. Fold in crab mixture and stir until heated through.

Allow to cool slightly. Place ¼ cup filling along centre of each crepe and roll up. Arrange fold-side down in a single layer in a baking dish. Top with remaining cheese and sprinkle with paprika. Heat in oven at 180°C (350°F) for 10–15 minutes. Garnish with parsley to serve.
Serves 16–18

Party Crab Crepes (above) and Creamy Crayfish Curry (below)

ROAST FRUIT DUCK WITH APRICOT CITRUS SAUCE

2.5 kg duck
2 cloves garlic, crushed
2 cups grated apple
12 pitted prunes
4 tablespoons breadcrumbs
1 egg
2 tablespoons brown sugar
salt and pepper, to taste
APRICOT CITRUS SAUCE
425 g can apricots, drained and chopped
½ cup white wine
juice and finely grated rind 1 orange
½ small onion, finely chopped

Preheat oven to 180°C (350°F). Wash duck and remove oil sacks from tail. Dry duck with paper towel and prick back several times with a skewer. Combine remaining ingredients and fill cavity with mixture. Secure opening with skewer.

Place duck on roasting rack in baking dish. Cook for 1 hour covered with lid or aluminium foil. Remove cover and bake additional 30–40 minutes. Cover and allow duck to stand 15 minutes before carving. Serve hot or cold.

To make sauce, combine all ingredients in pan, bring to boil then reduce heat and simmer 10 minutes. Pour into a sauce boat and serve.
Serves 6

CHICKEN WITH PLUM AND LYCHEE SAUCE

1.5 kg chicken, cut in bite-sized pieces
1 clove garlic, crushed
1 teaspoon minced ginger
1 tablespoon soy sauce
½ cup Chinese plum sauce
¼ teaspoon chilli sauce
1 tablespoon oil
¼ cup water chestnuts
¼ cup bamboo shoots, sliced
225 g can lychees, drained
¼ cup lychee juice
2 tablespoons cornflour
1 teaspoon sesame oil

Remove skin from chicken pieces. Marinate for 2 hours with garlic, ginger, soy, plum and chilli sauces. Drain and reserve liquid. Add sesame oil to wok, heat and stir-fry chicken pieces; cover with lid and simmer 5 minutes.

Add marinade juices. Cover and cook further 5 minutes. Add water chestnuts, bamboo shoots and lychees and stir-fry 1–2 minutes. Combine lychee juice and cornflour, add to wok and heat until thickened. Stir through sesame oil and serve hot with steamed rice.
Serves 6

SUMMER CHICKEN WITH CREAM AND TARRAGON SAUCE

1.5 kg chicken
60 g butter
2 teaspoons tarragon
juice 1 lemon
3 carrots, peeled and roughly chopped
1 onion, peeled and halved
1 bouquet garni
2 tablespoons dry vermouth
4 x 60 g eggs, separated
½ cup cream
salt and pepper, to taste
1 tablespoon Madeira
tarragon sprigs, to garnish

Rinse chicken with cold water and pat dry using absorbent paper. Beat together butter and tarragon until smooth and rub inside chicken cavity and just under skin. Rub lemon juice all over chicken. Place chicken in a large saucepan with carrots, onion, bouquet garni and dry vermouth. Add sufficient water to cover chicken. Place over a medium heat. Cover and simmer for 1½–1¾ hours. Remove chicken and place on a large plate to cool for 20 minutes then carve into large portions and remove skin.

Skim as much fat as possible from top of cooking liquid. Measure 2 cups of liquid, gradually add combined egg yolks and cream and beat well. Place in a double boiler and cook, stirring constantly until thickened. Season to taste and add Madeira.

Arrange chicken in a single layer in a shallow dish and spoon over sauce. Garnish with sprigs of fresh tarragon and refrigerate for at least 1 hour before serving.
Serves 6

Roast Fruit Duck with Apricot Citrus Sauce (above) and Chicken with Plum and Lychee Sauce (below)

Left to right: Fillets of Fish in Sangria Sauce and Stir-fried Beef and Mushrooms

FILLETS OF FISH IN SANGRIA SAUCE

12 whiting fillets
½ cup flour
salt and pepper, to taste
2 tablespoons lemon juice
60 g butter
juice ½ orange
1 tablespoon orange zest
¼ cup rose *or* white wine
2 egg yolks, beaten
cayenne pepper, to taste
¼ cup cream
1 tablespoon chopped parsley
5 g extra butter
peel from 1 orange, cut in fine strips
**   and blanched**

Coat fish fillets in combined flour, salt and pepper. Combine half the lemon juice and half the butter in frying pan. Heat till butter melts. Fry 6 fish fillets, 2 minutes on each side. Set fish fillets aside on platter.

Drain juices from pan. Heat remaining lemon juice and butter and fry remaining fish fillets. When cooked, place on serving platter, cover with aluminium foil and keep warm in oven.

Combine orange juice, zest and white wine in top of double saucepan. Bring to boil, then reduce heat to simmer. Add egg yolks and cayenne, stirring until thickened. Remove pan from heat.

Stir in cream, parsley and butter. Pour sauce over fish fillets and serve garnished with orange strips.
Serves 6

STIR-FRIED BEEF AND MUSHROOMS

5 dried Chinese mushrooms
500 g round steak, cut in slivers across
**   the grain**
2 cloves garlic, crushed
¼ teaspoon chopped ginger root
1 tablespoon soy sauce
2 tablespoons oyster sauce
1 tablespoon oil
125 g snow peas
2 stalks celery, sliced
3 leaves spinach, shredded
1 teaspoon sesame oil

Soak mushrooms in hot water for 20 minutes. Drain and discard stalks.

Combine steak, garlic, ginger, soy and oyster sauces. Marinate for 1 hour, drain and reserve liquid.

Heat oil in wok, add beef and fry till browned. Add marinade juices, fry for 3–5 minutes. Add mushrooms and cook for 2 minutes. Add snow peas and celery and fry 1 minute. Serve hot on spinach and sprinkle with sesame oil.
Serves 6

SLICED BEEF PLATTER WITH GREEN SAUCE

1–1.5 kg fillet of beef
salt and freshly ground pepper
90 g butter
¼ cup brandy
1 cup beef consomme
2 tablespoons sherry
1 tablespoon gelatine
125 g ham
1 tablespoon mayonnaise
pinch cayenne
1 egg, hard-boiled
1 stuffed green olive
1 shallot, to garnish
GREEN SAUCE
3 tablespoons finely chopped
 watercress
3 tablespoons finely chopped parsley
1 clove garlic, crushed
freshly ground pepper
4 capers, finely chopped
3 tablespoons olive oil
juice 1 lemon
salt, to taste

Trim fillet, remove all skin and tissue with a sharp knife. Rub meat with salt and pepper.

Melt butter in shallow pan. Saute fillet for 10 minutes or until brown on all sides. Warm brandy, ignite and pour over beef fillet. Cook until flame dies down.

Place fillet in a shallow roasting pan. Pour over pan juices. Bake at 200°C (400°F) for 15–20 minutes. Allow beef to cool. Chill in refrigerator.

Place consomme, sherry and gelatine in saucepan and bring to boil. Boil for 5 minutes. Remove ¾ cup soup and set aside. Pour remaining soup into shallow pan. Chill to set.

Puree ham till smooth. Fold in mayonnaise and cayenne. Spread cold beef with ham paste. Cut slices of egg white to form petals of a flower, arrange on beef. Slice stuffed olive to form centre of flower. Dip shallot into boiling water for 1 minute. Cut stems and leaves from green and arrange on beef.

Spoon cold gelatine glaze over beef. Chill well. Arrange beef on platter. Chop up remaining glaze and spoon around beef fillet. Serve with Green Sauce.

To make Green Sauce, combine watercress, parsley, garlic, pepper and capers in a small bowl. Add oil, drop by drop, beating constantly. Gradually add lemon juice and taste to adjust seasonings. Store in refrigerator in a screw-topped jar until ready to serve.
Serves 8

SHREDDED BARBECUE DUCK

2 kg duck
1 clove garlic, crushed
1 tablespoon sesame oil
1 tablespoon honey
1 tablespoon Hoi Sin sauce
1 tablespoon soy sauce
1 teaspoon chilli sauce
BARBECUE SAUCE
½ teaspoon finely grated ginger root
1 tablespoon light soy sauce
1 tablespoon honey
1 tablespoon dry sherry
1 tablespoon Hoi Sin sauce

Preheat oven to 190°C (375°F). Clean duck and dry with paper towel. Combine garlic, sesame oil, honey, Hoi Sin, soy and chilli sauces. Brush marinade over duck.

Place duck on rack in baking dish. Cover with aluminium foil and bake 1 hour brushing occasionally with marinade. Remove foil, and bake a further 30–40 minutes or until cooked when tested.

Allow duck to stand 15 minutes before slicing into thin strips. Joint legs and wings. Serve duck arranged in layers on platter with wings and legs at end of platter. Serve hot or cold. To make sauce, combine all ingredients in a pan, heat through and serve in a sauce boat.
Serves 6

PORK AND PINEAPPLE HOTPOT

60 g butter
1.5 kg pork fillet, diced
220 g can pineapple pieces, drained
2 green capsicums, seeded
1 cup chopped celery
220 g can champignons, drained
1 red chilli, diced
1 cup white wine
salt and pepper, to taste
1 cup chicken stock
3 tablespoons cornflour
2 tablespoons chopped parsley

Melt butter in a large saucepan, add pork and cook 10 minutes turning constantly. Add pineapple, capsicum, celery, champignons and chilli. Cook 1 minute, stirring to combine. Add wine, salt and pepper and simmer 20 minutes. In a separate bowl combine stock, cornflour and parsley. Add to casserole and cook over medium heat 10 minutes, stirring occasionally. Serve with boiled rice.
Serves 6

VEAL WITH TUNA SAUCE

1.2 kg veal (a boned piece of leg is
 ideal)
1 carrot
1 onion
2 celery stalks
1 strip lemon *or* orange peel
⅔ cup white wine
⅔ cup olive oil
salt, to taste
200 g can tuna in oil
4 anchovy fillets
1½ cups home-made mayonnaise
1 tablespoon capers
3 gherkins

Roll up meat and secure with string or toothpicks to maintain its shape. Place it in a deep casserole or pan with carrot, onion, celery, a strip of lemon peel, wine, olive oil and 300 mL cold water. Salt lightly and cook in the oven or on top of the stove for 1 hour or until veal is done. Lift it out and allow to cool.

Strain cooking liquid and let it reduce until well concentrated. Place contents of tin of tuna in a food processor, together with a little of the reduced cooking broth and anchovy fillets. Let it whirl around for 1 minute then add resulting mixture to home-made mayonnaise. You should obtain a rather runny sauce: if too thick, add a few more spoons of cooking liquid.

Slice meat and arrange slices on a serving platter. Pour sauce on top and decorate with capers and sliced gherkins. Refrigerate before serving.
Serves 4

Clockwise from top left: Shredded Barbecue Duck; Sliced Beef Platter with Green Sauce; Veal with Tuna Sauce

Some Festive Favourites

ROAST TURKEY WITH HERB STUFFING

5–6 kg turkey
HERB STUFFING
185 g butter, melted
2 teaspoons salt
½ teaspoon fresh sage
½ teaspoon fresh thyme
pepper, to taste
4 cups soft bread cubes
¾ cup milk
2 stalks celery, chopped
1 small onion, chopped
BASTE
¼ cup orange juice
60 g butter, melted

Rinse turkey and pat dry with paper towel.

To make herb stuffing, combine all ingredients in a large bowl, adjust seasoning to taste.

Fill turkey cavity with stuffing and sew or skewer openings. Secure drumsticks under skin at tail. Place, breast side up, on rack in roasting pan. Brush turkey with baste (orange juice and butter combined), cover with aluminium foil and bake at 175°C (340°F) for 3 hours.

Remove foil, baste again and continue cooking a further 30 minutes–1 hour to brown. Cover and allow turkey to stand 20 minutes before carving. Serve hot or cold.
Serves 12

ROAST GOOSE WITH APPLE AND PRUNE STUFFING

6 kg goose
APPLE AND PRUNE STUFFING
2 cups pitted prunes
3 large cooking apples, peeled, cored and quartered
squeeze lemon juice
freshly ground pepper, to taste
BASTE
3 tablespoons chicken stock
2 tablespoons Calvados or brandy
¼ cup apple juice
freshly ground pepper

Preheat oven to 180°C (350°F). Rinse goose, remove oil sacs from tail, pat dry and prick back with skewer.

To prepare Apple and Prune Stuffing, combine all ingredients in a bowl, adjust seasoning to taste.

Fill cavity with stuffing and secure opening with skewers. Place, breast side down, on rack in roasting pan. Brush turkey with baste (stock, calvados, apple juice and pepper combined), and cover with aluminium foil.

Bake for 3 hours. Drain away excess fat from pan twice. Turn goose breast side up and baste with remaining mixture. Roast uncovered further 30 minutes–1 hour. Cover and allow to stand 20 minutes before carving. Serve hot or cold.
Serves 12

BOILED FRUIT CAKE

1 cup water
1 cup brown sugar
250 g butter
1½ cups raisins, chopped
3 cups sultanas
1⅔ cups currants
1 cup glace cherries, chopped
⅓ cup mixed peel
⅓ cup glace pineapple, chopped
½ teaspoon cinnamon
½ teaspoon nutmeg
½ teaspoon ginger
½ teaspoon allspice
1 teaspoon bicarbonate of soda
3 eggs
2 cups self-raising flour
1 cup flour
¼ cup rum or dry sherry

Preheat oven to 180°C (350°F).

In large saucepan place water, brown sugar, butter, all the fruits, spices and bicarbonate of soda. Cook over low heat to melt butter and blend ingredients. Allow to cool. Add eggs and flours and mix evenly.

Place mixture in double-lined 20 cm square cake tin. (Use buttered brown paper, cutting paper 5 cm taller than tin.) Bake for 1½–2 hours.

Insert wooden skewer to test whether cake is cooked. When cooked carefully turn out on cake rack and remove paper from base and sides. Drizzle rum over warm cake. Allow to cool completely. Wrap in greaseproof paper and aluminium foil to store.

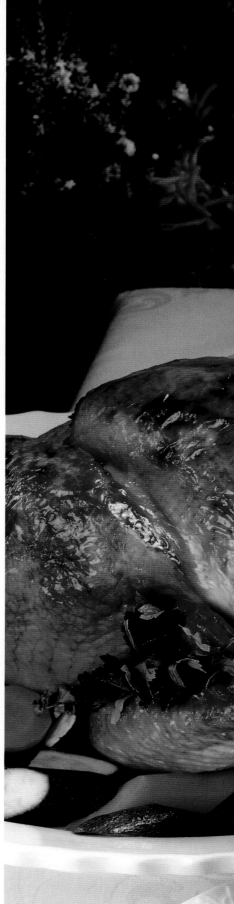

Clockwise from left: Roast Turkey with Herb Stuffing; Baked Mustard Ham; Christmas Pudding in a Cloth; Boiled Fruit Cake; Fruit Mince Delight

PORK ROAST WITH CHERRY SAUCE

3–4 kg pork loin
2 tablespoons cooking oil
1 tablespoon coarse salt
6 cloves garlic
12 small bay leaves
CHERRY SAUCE
½ cup pitted cherries
¼ cup corn syrup
2 tablespoons vinegar
salt and pepper, to taste
pinch nutmeg
pinch cinnamon
pinch ground cloves

Deeply score rind of pork into 1.5 cm strips. Place pork loin, skin side down, in a pan and pour in 2 cups boiling water. Bake at 210°C (410°F) for 15 minutes. Remove pan and drain off liquid, reserving it for basting.

Add oil to pan. Rub pork skin with salt. Insert cloves and bay leaves in score marks. Roast pork, skin side up at 190°C (375°F) for 3–3½ hours. Baste with drained liquid every 30 minutes. When cooked remove from pan, cover and allow to stand for 20 minutes before carving.

In saucepan, combine sauce ingredients, bring to boil and cook for 3 minutes until heated through.

Carve pork and serve sliced on platter with Cherry Sauce.
Serves 12

BAKED MUSTARD HAM

3–4 kg pickled leg of ham
1 bay leaf
6 peppercorns
2 tablespoons sherry
4 tablespoons coarse-grain mustard
1 tablespoon apricot jam

Place ham in large boiler and cover with water. Add bay leaf, peppercorns and sherry. Cover with lid and bring to boil. Reduce heat and simmer for 2 hours then allow meat to cool in liquid and drain.

Combine mustard and apricot jam. Spread over surface of ham. Place ham on rack in baking pan and cover with aluminium foil. Bake in oven at 180°C (350°F) for 1 hour. Remove foil and continue baking 45 minutes. Remove from oven and allow to cool. Serve in fine slices.
Serves 10

Pork Roast with Cherry Sauce

Gran's Traditional Christmas Cake and Christmas Fruit Topping

GRAN'S TRADITIONAL CHRISTMAS CAKE

500 g butter
2 cups brown sugar
10 eggs
1 cup glace cherries, chopped
½ cup mixed peel
3 cups sultanas
3½ cups currants
1½ cups raisins, chopped
½ tablespoon allspice
¼ cup rum
1 teaspoon vanilla
¼ cup milk
5 cups flour
½ tablespoon baking powder

ALMOND PASTE
1 cup ground almonds
⅓ cup icing sugar
¼ cup caster sugar
1 egg white
ICING
2 egg whites
500 g icing sugar
1 teaspoon glycerine
2 teaspoons lemon juice
food colouring (optional)

Preheat oven to 160°C (325°F). Cream butter and sugar until smooth. Add eggs one at a time and beat mixture for 5 minutes. Add fruits, spice, rum, vanilla and milk. Lastly add sifted flour and baking powder and blend.

Spoon mixture into a double-lined 23 cm round or square cake tin. Carefully bang tin twice on benchtop to release air pockets from cake mix. Bake for 5–5½ hours. Insert wooden skewer to test if cake is cooked.

Stand on cake rack and cool cake in tin ½–1 hour before inverting onto cake rack to cool. Leave lining paper on cake. When cold, wrap in greaseproof paper and aluminium foil to store. Decorate cake with icing or Christmas fruit.
Almond paste Blend together ground almonds and both sugars in a bowl. Stir in egg white and knead mixture to a smooth, thick paste. Dust a board with a little icing sugar and roll paste out to form a circle to fit top of cake.
Icing Beat egg whites until frothy. Add sugar gradually, beating after each addition. Lastly add glycerine and lemon juice and beat for several minutes.

Divide icing, using white icing on top and sides of cake and colouring a small amount for decoration.

CHRISTMAS PUDDING IN A CLOTH

1½ cups raisins, chopped
½ cup blanched almonds, chopped
½ cup pitted dates, chopped
⅓ cup glace cherries, chopped
⅓ cup mixed peel
1½ cups sultanas
1⅔ cups currants
1 small apple, peeled and grated
½ cup rum or brandy
250 g butter
1 cup brown sugar
4 eggs

1 cup flour
pinch salt
3 teaspoons allspice
½ teaspoon bicarbonate of soda
2½ cups soft white breadcrumbs
custard, brandy butter *or* cream, to
serve

Combine chopped raisins, almonds, dates and cherries in a large bowl. Add mixed peel, sultanas, currants and apple. Pour over rum, cover and allow to stand overnight.

Cream butter and sugar. Add eggs beating well. Sift flour, salt, mixed spice and bicarbonate of soda. Add breadcrumbs to flour mixture. Fold flour, butter and fruit mixtures together. Dip pudding cloth in boiling water. Squeeze out excess moisture and lay cloth flat. Sift plenty of flour over three-quarters of cloth and rub in well — this forms a seal which prevents water seeping into pudding during cooking. Spoon mixture onto centre of cloth and bring up sides of material. Secure well with string.

Bring approximately 2 litres water to boil. Lower pudding into water. Cover and boil pudding 4 hours, adding hot water as necessary. Remove pudding, drain and hang for 1 day. Reheat by boiling 2 hours. Remove from cloth. Serve with custard, brandy butter or cream.
Serves 12

1 Sift flour over damp pudding cloth

2 Rub in flour well to form a seal

3 Spoon pudding mixture into centre

4 Form a pudding shape with mixture

5 Bring up sides of cloth around pudding

6 Secure well with string

1 Grate half the dough into a lamington tin

2 Spread fruit mince evenly over pastry base

3 Grate remaining dough on top to cover mince

FRUIT-MINCE DELIGHT

PASTRY
2⅓ cups flour
1 teaspoon cinnamon
salt, to taste
180 g butter
½ cup caster sugar
1 egg, lightly beaten

FRUIT MINCE
1½ cups mixed dried fruit
440 g can crushed pineapple and juice
1 cooking apple, peeled, cored and grated
1 cup brown sugar
1 teaspoon nutmeg
1 tablespoon cornflour *blended with*
1 tablespoon pineapple juice

Sift flour, cinnamon and salt into a bowl. Rub in butter to resemble breadcrumbs. Stir in sugar and egg to form dough. Knead lightly then wrap in plastic and refrigerate 1 hour. Grate half the dough over base of 30 × 20 cm lamington tin. Press down lightly and evenly with the back of a spoon. Set aside. Preheat oven to 180°C (350°F).

Place mixed fruit, pineapple and juice, apple, sugar and nutmeg in saucepan. Add cornflour paste and simmer until thickened. Cool slightly. Spread fruit mince over pastry base. Grate remaining dough over top to completely cover mince. Bake 35–40 minutes or until golden brown. Cool on wire rack. Cut into bars.

Makes 12–16

Brunches and Lunches

Whether you are gathering together a few close friends or a crowd, brunches and lunches are a great way to entertain — indoors or out.

Here we include recipes for just about any midday menu imaginable, from light and luscious mains to barbecue specials, party-time pies plus breads and salads and the sweetest treats imaginable for afters.

Light and Luscious Mains

RICE SALAD WITH PRAWNS AND MUSSELS

200 g rice
500 g freshly cooked king prawns
1 kg mussels
½ cup dry white wine
2 lemons
6 tablespoons olive oil
pepper, to taste
1 small bunch parsley, finely chopped
3 anchovy fillets, chopped

Brush mussels under running water to free shells of grit. Discard any open ones. Put them in a wide pan with wine and bring to boil. Lift them out as soon as they open. Shell approximately half of them, reserving the other half for decoration. Shell prawns.

Boil rice in salted water, drain it and run some cold water through it to separate grains. Season it with juice of half a lemon, oil, plenty of pepper, parsley and anchovy fillets. Add salt if necessary.

Just before serving, stir prawns into rice, reserving some for decoration. Arrange rice in a glass bowl and decorate it with reserved prawns, mussels in shell and lemon slices. Serve very cold.
Serves 4

PAELLA

¼ cup olive oil
1 kg chicken fillets, cut in chunks
2 onions, chopped
2 cloves garlic, crushed
125 g minced pork
2 tomatoes, peeled and chopped
300 g packet frozen peas
320 g can artichoke hearts, drained and cut up
2 teaspoons paprika
1½ cups rice
2 teaspoons salt
4 cups chicken stock
1 packet saffron threads soaked in eggcupful boiling water
500 g uncooked prawns, peeled and deveined
12 mussels, scrubbed
12 black olives

Heat oil in a deep-frying pan. Cook chicken, onion and garlic until brown. Add pork and brown quickly. Add tomatoes, peas, artichokes, paprika and rice. Cook, stirring until rice is well coated with oil. Add salt, stock and saffron and cook for 15 minutes until rice is almost tender. Add prawns and mussels and continue cooking until prawns turn pink and mussels open. Garnish with olives.
Note: If preparing in advance, do not add prawns and mussels until just before serving as they may toughen.
Serves 8

Clockwise from left: Barbecue Fillet of Beef with Horseradish Cream; Mushroom Quiche; Prawns with Creamy Sate Sauce

SEAFOOD PLATTER WITH TWO SPICY SAUCES

BEER BATTER
3 cups flour
pinch salt
2 eggs, separated
2 cups beer
1 cup milk
60 g butter, melted
oil, for deep-frying

SEAFOOD PLATTER
1.5 kg fish fillets (gemfish, whiting)
250 g calamari rings
500 g uncooked prawns, shelled and deveined
250 g scallops
lemon twists *and* parsley, to garnish

MANGO SEAFOOD SAUCE
1 small mango, peeled, seeded and sliced
1 cup sour cream
¼ cup natural mayonnaise *(see note)*
2 teaspoons finely grated onion
1 tablespoon finely chopped coriander

LEMON MAYONNAISE
1 cup mayonnaise
2 tablespoons lemon juice
1 tablespoon finely chopped parsley
1 teaspoon finely chopped capers
freshly ground pepper

Sift flour and salt into a bowl. Make a well in the centre and add egg yolks. Stir in a little of the surrounding flour. Combine beer, milk and melted butter. Gradually add beer mixture, beating until smooth then strain. Allow mixture to stand for at least 30 minutes. Whisk egg white until stiff and fold into batter. Use at once.

Check fish fillets for bones. Heat oil for deep-frying. Dip a few pieces of the seafood at a time into the batter. Cook 6 pieces of seafood at a time until golden brown and cooked through. Drain on paper towel and serve garnished with lemon twists and parsley.

To make Mango Seafood Sauce, place mango in a food processor and puree or press through a sieve using the back of a wooden spoon. Combine with remaining ingredients and beat until smooth. Taste and adjust seasonings if desired. Serve immediately in a sauce boat.

To make Lemon Mayonnaise, combine all ingredients in a small bowl and mix until thoroughly blended. Taste and adjust seasonings if desired. Serve in a sauce boat.

Note: Natural mayonnaise has no preservatives or artificial food colourings. It can be purchased from delicatessens and supermarkets.
Serves 10

ALMOND FRIED CHICKEN WITH SPICED GINGER SAUCE

2 kg chicken pieces
⅔ cup grated Parmesan cheese
⅓ cup dry breadcrumbs
¼ cup ground almonds
salt and pepper, to taste
2 eggs
1 tablespoon milk
⅓ cup flour
oil, for frying

SPICED GINGER SAUCE
1 tablespoon finely grated ginger root
1 teaspoon whole allspice
1 teaspoon whole peppercorns
½ teaspoon mustard seed
½ teaspoon whole cloves
⅔ cup dry white wine
3 tablespoons white wine vinegar
2 tablespoons soy sauce

Remove skin from chicken pieces. Pat dry with paper towel. Combine Parmesan, breadcrumbs, almonds, salt and pepper. Set aside. Blend together eggs and milk.

Dip chicken pieces in flour then egg mixture then almond mixture. Heat oil in frying pan. Fry chicken portions in oil, turning to brown all sides. Fry gently 10 minutes. Drain on paper towel and serve hot or cold.

To make Spiced Ginger Sauce, combine ginger and spices in a mortar and pestle and crush lightly. If you do not have a mortar and pestle, place on a sheet of aluminium foil, fold the foil over and crush with a rolling pin. Combine white wine, vinegar and soy sauce in a small saucepan. Add spices and gently heat until boiling. Boil for 8 minutes then strain. Serve sauce in a shallow bowl suitable for dipping.
Serves 6

Left to right: Almond Fried Chicken with Spiced Ginger Sauce; Seafood Platter with Two Spicy Sauces

CHICKEN AND CHEESE SALAD WITH ITALIAN DRESSING

3 cups torn endive
½ head lettuce, torn
3 hard-boiled eggs, peeled and sliced
½ cup sliced radishes
2 tomatoes, peeled, chilled and
    quartered
1 cup cooked chicken strips
1 cup Swiss cheese strips
¼ cup thinly sliced ham
¼ cup thinly sliced tongue
¼ cup thinly sliced salami
½ cup Italian dressing
anchovy fillets, to garnish

Combine endive, lettuce, egg and radish slices. Halve mixture. Place half endive mixture in row on square platter. Place tomato wedges next to endive mixture in row. Combine chicken and cheese strips and arrange in a row alongside tomatoes. Put rest of endive mixture beside chicken and cheese. Complete salad platter with combined mixture of ham, tongue and salami. Coat each row lightly with salad dressing and garnish with anchovy fillets.
Serves 6

SALMON MOUSSE

1 cup loosely packed fresh dill sprigs
1 cup mayonnaise
2 cups low-fat yoghurt
1 tablespoon gelatine
3 teaspoons lemon juice
2 slices onion
½ teaspoon paprika
450 g tinned salmon
freshly ground pepper, to taste
dash Tabasco sauce
1 cucumber, peeled and sliced, to
    garnish

Chop dill and place two-thirds in a small bowl with ½ cup mayonnaise and 1 cup yoghurt. Chill to serve as garnish with cucumber slices when mousse is ready.

Add gelatine, lemon juice, onion and ½ cup boiling water to remaining dill. Blend to dissolve gelatine. Add remaining mayonnaise and yoghurt with all remaining ingredients and blend again.

Rinse mould in cold water but do not dry. Pour in mixture and chill overnight. Serve with cucumber garnish slices.
Serves 6–8

TURKEY AND ROQUEFORT SALAD WITH CRANBERRY DRESSING

1 cup shredded lettuce
3 cups diced cooked turkey
1 cup diced celery
½ cup seedless grapes
½ cup toasted pecans, chopped
45 g Roquefort cheese, crumbled

CRANBERRY DRESSING
250 g jar cranberry sauce
¼ cup dark soy sauce
1 small clove garlic, crushed
2 tablespoons lemon juice
2 tablespoons sherry
1 tablespoon vegetable oil

Combine lettuce, turkey, celery, grapes and pecans. Pile mixture into shallow serving dish. Crumble Roquefort cheese over top of salad.

To make Cranberry Dressing, combine all ingredients in a small saucepan and heat until well blended. Serve separately in a sauce boat.
Serves 6

Turkey and Roquefort Salad with Cranberry Dressing

MARINATED LAMB SALAD

750 g roast lamb, trimmed of fat and cut in strips
½ cup olive oil
1 cup red wine vinegar
3 tablespoons honey
1½ teaspoons salt
pinch dry mustard
2 teaspoons dried mint
¼ teaspoon oregano
¼ teaspoon thyme
¼ teaspoon anise seed
1 cucumber, peeled and sliced
4 tomatoes, quartered
½ bunch curly endive
1 cup pitted black olives

Combine lamb with olive oil, vinegar, honey, salt, mustard, mint leaves and herbs. Refrigerate for 1 hour.

Line serving dish with cucumber, tomato quarters and curly endive. Drain lamb strips, reserving dressing. Spoon lamb strips into centre of dish. Combine dressing and olives. Pour over meat and vegetables to serve.
Serves 6

Marinated Lamb Salad

Barbecue Specials

BARBECUED FISH

2 × 1.5–2 kg whole cleaned fish (whiting, bream *or* mullet)
2 lemons
salt and freshly ground pepper, to taste
3 onions, sliced in rings
250 g mushrooms, sliced
4 tomatoes, sliced
80 g butter
lemon wedges, to serve

Remove scales and wipe fish with a damp cloth. Peel rind from 1 lemon, cut into julienne strips and simmer for a few minutes; drain and cool. Sqeeze lemons and brush lemon juice over both fish. Season with salt and pepper. Place fish on 2 large pieces of aluminium foil, shiny side down. Spread onion rings over both fish, then cover with mushrooms and tomatoes. Season with pepper and dot butter over fish. Drizzle over any remaining lemon juice and sprinkle with rind. Wrap fish in foil, forming a seal on 1 side.

Cook fish over glowing coals for 25–40 minutes or until cooked when tested. (Cooking time will depend on heat of fire and thickness of fish.) Serve fish with the vegetables and cooking juices. Garnish with lemon wedges.
Serves 10–12

BARBECUED FILLET OF BEEF WITH HORSERADISH CREAM SAUCE

1.5 kg fillet beef
4–6 rashers bacon, rinds removed
MARINADE
1 carrot, roughly chopped
1 onion, roughly chopped
1 cup port
½ cup oil
few peppercorns
1 teaspoon whole allspice
1 clove garlic, crushed

HORSERADISH CREAM SAUCE
1 cup thickened cream, whipped and chilled
1 tablespoon horseradish cream
1 shallot, finely chopped
1 tablespoon finely chopped parsley

Trim fillet of excess fat and all sinew. Place on a board and wrap bacon around in a spiral fashion. Secure with toothpicks. Combine all marinade ingredients and place with fillet in a strong plastic bag. Secure bag opening and ensure fillet is covered with marinade. Refrigerate overnight turning bag from time to time. Remove fillet from marinade and pat dry with paper towel.

Cook fillet over moderately hot barbecue coals for about 10–12 minutes for a medium rare steak or 15–20 minutes for a medium steak. Test with a skewer then remove from barbecue and stand meat for 10 minutes before carving. Carve thin slices across the grain. Arrange on a platter and serve with Horseradish Cream Sauce.

To make sauce, combine all ingredients, stir until blended and serve in a bowl.
Serves 10

Left to right above: Prawns with Creamy Sate Sauce and Barbecue Fillet of Beef with Horseradish Cream; below: Tandoori Chicken; Prawns with Creamy Sate Sauce; Barbecued Fish

HONEYED LAMB KEBABS

1.5 kg lean lamb, trimmed and diced
¼ cup white wine
2 tablespoons Hoi Sin sauce
2 tablespoons sherry
2 tablespoons honey
1 clove garlic, crushed
salt and freshly ground pepper, to taste
1 large onion, cut into wedges

Marinate lamb in combined wine, Hoi Sin sauce, sherry, honey and garlic. Season, cover and refrigerate overnight. Drain and reserve marinade to use as a baste during cooking.

Soak sate sticks in boiling water to cover for 10 minutes. Drain and thread lamb dice onto sate sticks interspersed with wedges of onion. Cook kebabs under a preheated hot grill or over a barbecue, basting occasionally with marinade. Turn to cook and brown each side.
Serves 6-8

MINTY LAMB BURGERS

2.5-3 kg boned leg of lamb
2 onions, finely chopped
1-2 cloves garlic, crushed
2 tablespoons chopped mint
1 teaspoon paprika
salt and freshly ground pepper, to taste
3 eggs, beaten
TO SERVE
250 g butter
2-3 tablespoons chopped mint

Trim all skin and visible fat off lamb then cut into pieces. Mince, using a food processor or mincer. Avoid processing the lamb too finely.

Place mince in a bowl with onions, garlic, mint, paprika, salt, pepper and eggs and mix well. Cover and refrigerate.

Beat butter until soft. Add mint and beat again. Taste for mint flavour and add freshly ground pepper. Spoon butter onto a sheet of foil and roll into a log shape. Refrigerate until serving time.

Divide lamb mixture into 20 parts. With wet hands, shape each into a burger shape. Cook over glowing coals for 5-10 minutes until done. Serve burgers topped with a thin slice of mint butter.
Serves 10-12

Minty Lamb Burgers

TANDOORI CHICKEN

16-20 chicken pieces
2 large onions, grated
3 cloves garlic, crushed
juice 3 lemons
1 teaspoon salt
1½ cups natural yoghurt
1½ tablespoons ground coriander
2 teaspoons turmeric
2 teaspoons ground chilli
2 teaspoons black mustard seeds, ground
1 teaspoon red food colouring powder

Remove skin from chicken and prick flesh several times with a skewer. Mix onions, garlic, lemon juice and salt. Rub all over the chicken and leave for 30 minutes.

Combine yoghurt, spices and food colouring. Pour yoghurt mixture over chicken, stirring to coat all pieces. Cover and marinate for at least 12 hours in the refrigerator. Cook chicken over glowing coals for 20-30 minutes or until cooked.
Serves 10-12

PRAWNS WITH CREAMY SATE SAUCE

½ cup peanut butter
1 clove garlic, crushed
2 tablespoons light soy sauce
finely grated rind and juice 1 lemon
1 teaspoon dried prawn paste
1-2 red chillies, seeded and finely chopped
½ cup cream
1 kg uncooked prawns, shelled, deveined, with tails on

Combine all ingredients except cream and prawns, in a small saucepan. Stir over gentle heat until well blended. Remove from heat and stir in cream.

Soak 20 bamboo skewers in boiling water for 10 minutes (this will prevent them burning when barbecuing). Thread prawns onto skewers and cook over hot coals basting frequently with sauce. Serve with any remaining sauce.
Serves 10

The Party-time Pie Shop

CHICKEN AND MUSHROOM PIE

1.5 kg chicken
2 tablespoons dry sherry
6 black peppercorns
½ tablespoon chopped fresh herbs
¼ teaspoon sage
½ teaspoon salt
¼ cup sliced leek
½ cup chopped onion
1 clove garlic, crushed
60 g butter
250 g fresh mushrooms, sliced
freshly ground pepper
12 sheets filo pastry
90 g butter, melted
1 tablespoon sesame seeds

Clean and rinse chicken. Place in large saucepan with sherry, peppercorns, herbs and salt. Cover with cold water and bring to boil. Simmer for 45 minutes. Allow to cool in liquid then drain, discarding stock.

Remove skin and bones from chicken and discard. Cut up chicken meat and set aside.

Saute leek, onion and garlic in butter until transparent. Add mushrooms and pepper and cook 2 minutes. Add mushroom mixture to chicken meat, stirring to blend. Place chicken mixture in 20 cm pie plate.

Cut pastry sheets in half to cover top of pie plate. Place between 2 dry tea towels and cover with a just damp tea towel to keep pastry moist. Layer pastry over filling, brushing every second sheet with butter. Roughly tuck pastry around edge of dish. Brush with butter and sprinkle with sesame seeds.

Bake on top shelf at 200°C (400°F) for 45 minutes or until golden brown. Serve hot.
Serves 6–8

MUSHROOM QUICHE

375 g ready-rolled frozen shortcrust pastry, thawed
40 g butter
1 large onion, finely chopped
1 clove garlic, crushed
375 g button mushrooms, sliced
juice ½ lemon
4 eggs
1½ cups cream
salt and freshly ground pepper, to taste

Halve pastry, roll out and line 2 × 23 cm flan tins. Preheat oven to 200°C (400°F). Place greaseproof paper over pastry and weigh down with rice grains. Bake blind for 10 minutes. Remove paper and rice and bake pastry a further 5 minutes then set aside.

Heat butter and saute onion and garlic for 5 minutes. Add mushrooms and saute 3–5 minutes. Off the heat add lemon juice.

Beat eggs, add cream and beat again. Season with salt and pepper. Spoon mushrooms onto pastry bases then pour over cream mixture. Bake quiches for 15 minutes. Reduce temperature to 180°C (350°F) and bake a further 20–25 minutes until cooked when tested. Allow to cool then serve sliced.
Serves 12

BACON AND ASPARAGUS QUICHE

PASTRY
1¾ cups flour
salt, to taste
60 g butter
1 egg yolk, beaten
cold water

FILLING
2 rashers bacon, chopped and rind removed
2 shallots, chopped
20 g butter
5 eggs
100 mL cream
60 g grated Cheddar cheese
15 g blue vein cheese, crumbled
1 medium-sized tomato, sliced
8–10 canned asparagus spears

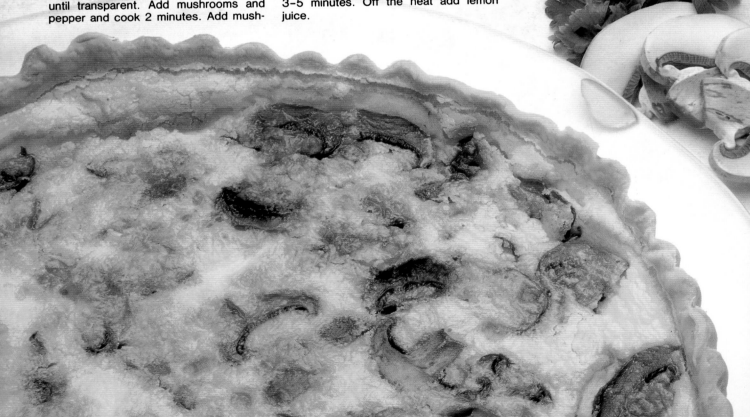

Preheat oven to 220°C (425°F).

Sift flour and salt into a bowl and rub in butter to resemble breadcrumbs.

Stir in egg yolk and sufficient water to form soft dough. Knead dough on lightly floured board. Roll out to fit 23 cm flan tin, trimming to fit. Prick base of pastry and bake blind for 10 minutes.

Saute bacon, shallots and butter for 2 minutes. Beat eggs and cream together, then strain. Fold in grated cheeses and bacon mixture.

Place tomato slices on pastry base, top with asparagus spears and pour over egg mixture. Reduce oven temperature to 190°C (375°F) and bake for 45 minutes or until set and browned on top. Serve hot or cold.
Serves 6–8

VEGETARIAN PIE

PASTRY
1½ cups flour
¼ teaspoon baking powder
pinch salt
2 teaspoons curry powder
125 g butter
2 tablespoons chopped onion

FILLING
250 g spinach, washed and chopped
1 onion, chopped
20 g butter
225 g can mixed beans, drained
200 g can creamed corn
1 tablespoon chopped parsley
1 teaspoon salt
1 tablespoon tomato sauce
dash Tabasco sauce
600 g cottage cheese
1 egg
paprika, to taste

Preheat oven to 200°C (400°F). Sift flour, baking powder, salt and curry powder into a bowl. Rub in butter to resemble breadcrumbs. Add onion and sufficient water to form dough. Knead dough lightly on floured board. Roll out to fit 23 cm flan dish. Trim edges and prick with fork. Bake blind for 10 minutes.

Saute spinach and onion in butter over low heat for 2 minutes. Drain excess liquid. Layer spinach, onion, mixed beans, creamed corn and parsley on base. Combine salt, tomato sauce, Tabasco, cottage cheese and egg. Pour over vegetable filling and sprinkle with paprika. Return to oven and bake for 30 minutes. Serve hot or cold.
Serves 6

Clockwise from top: Chicken and Mushroom Pie; Bacon and Asparagus Quiche; Mushroom Quiche

Salads on the side

GREEN SALAD WITH DIJON MUSTARD DRESSING

3 cups torn spinach
½ head lettuce, torn
4 stalks celery, chopped
½ green capsicum, diced
1 cucumber, rinsed and sliced
2 tablespoons chopped chives
6 green olives, pitted and sliced
1 avocado, pitted, peeled and sliced

DIJON MUSTARD DRESSING
1 tablespoon vinegar
2 tablespoons vegetable oil
1 teaspoon Dijon mustard
freshly ground pepper

Wash and drain spinach and lettuce and combine with celery and capsicum. Place row of cucumber slices around edge of salad dish. Sprinkle chives over.

To make dressing, combine all ingredients in a screw-topped jar and shake well.

Toss spinach mixture with dressing, pile into centre of serving dish and garnish salad with olives and avocado slices.
Serves 6

MARINATED CUCUMBER AND ONION

2 medium-sized cucumbers, peeled and sliced
2 teaspoons salt
3 tablespoons white vinegar
3 tablespoons water
½ teaspoon sugar
¼ teaspoon paprika
¼ teaspoon pepper
½ clove garlic, crushed
6 shallots, sliced, to serve

Place cucumber slices in a shallow bowl. Combine salt, vinegar, water, sugar, paprika, pepper and garlic and pour over cucumber slices, tossing lightly to coat. Cover and chill in refrigerator for 3 hours. Garnish with sliced shallots to serve.
Serves 6

AVOCADO AND LETTUCE SALAD WITH MUSTARD SEED DRESSING

1 lettuce
2 avocados, peeled, sliced and sprinkled with
juice ½ lemon
1 small cucumber, peeled and sliced
6 shallots, trimmed
alfalfa sprouts

MUSTARD SEED DRESSING
2 tablespoons natural yoghurt
1 tablespoon vegetable oil
2 teaspoons mustard seeds
1 teaspoons grated ginger root

Wash and dry lettuce. Refrigerate 30 minutes until crisp then tear into bite-sized pieces. Place in salad bowl. Top with avocado slices. Add cucumber and garnish with shallots and alfalfa sprouts.

To make dressing, combine all ingredients mixing until smooth. Just before serving pour over salad and toss.
Serves 8–10

CITRUS AND MANGO SALAD WITH CREAM DRESSING

1 lettuce
3 oranges, peeled and white pith removed
3 stalks celery, cut into 8 cm pieces
450 g can mango slices, drained
1 cucumber, scored and sliced
6 shallots, finely sliced

CREAM DRESSING
¼ cup mayonnaise
½ cup cream
salt and freshly ground pepper
2 tablespoons chopped parsley
1 teaspoon French mustard
3 teaspoons orange juice
2 teaspoons lemon juice

Wash lettuce and arrange leaves on a serving plate. Segment the oranges. To make celery curls, slice the celery lengthways leaving one end uncut. Drop celery into iced water until it curls.

Arrange mango slices, orange segments, celery curls and cucumber between lettuce leaves. Garnish with shallots and refrigerate until ready to serve.

To make dressing, mix all ingredients well, stand 15–20 minutes before using and serve separately.
Serves 6–8

EXOTIC FLOWER SALAD

1 large mango
1 tablespoon lemon juice
1 tablespoon salad oil
salt, to taste
125 g button mushrooms, finely sliced
freshly ground pepper
1 large lettuce
1 tablespoon chopped herbs
2 tablespoons pine nuts, toasted
60 g snowpeas, topped, tailed and blanched
1 witloof, separated into leaves
1 quantity Creamy Vinaigrette Dressing (see recipe)

Peel the mango and cut a thick slice from each side of stone and set aside for the salad. Cut remaining flesh from stone and puree. Add lemon juice, oil and salt. Combine the mushrooms and pepper, and toss lightly.

Arrange lettuce leaves on plates in a flower shape with the mushrooms in middle. Sprinkle over the chopped herbs and nuts, arrange mango slices, snowpeas and witloof on the plate. Drizzle Creamy Vinaigrette Dressing on top and serve.
Serves 6

RED CABBAGE NUT SLAW WITH TAHINI ORANGE DRESSING

3 cups shredded red cabbage
1 cup shredded green cabbage
½ cup whole toasted blanched almonds

BASE DRESSING
2 tablespoons cream
1 tablespoons tarragon vinegar
1 teaspoon prepared mustard
¼ teaspoon garlic salt

TAHINI ORANGE DRESSING
2 tablespoons tahini
2 tablespoons water
juice and finely grated rind 1 orange

Combine red and green cabbage, wash, drain and chill in refrigerator. Combine base dressing ingredients in a screw-top jar and shake well. Toss cabbage with dressing and ¼ cup almonds. Pile into salad bowl and top with remaining almonds. To serve, spoon over Tahini Orange Dressing.
Serves 6

Clockwise from top: Avocado and Lettuce Salad with Mustard Seed Dressing; Red Cabbage Nut Slaw with Tahini Orange Dressing; Green Salad with Dijon Mustard Dressing

The Bread Board

PATAFLA

1 baguette or other long French loaf
6 tomatoes, peeled and chopped
1 onion, finely chopped
6 shallots, finely chopped
2 green capsicums, seeded and
    chopped
1 red capsicum, seeded and chopped
250 g black olives, pitted and chopped
3 tablespoons capers
3 gherkins, chopped
freshly ground pepper, to taste
3 tablespoons olive oil

Halve the loaf lengthways and scoop out
the crumb. Place crumb in a bowl with
vegetables, olives, capers and gherkins,
beat mixture well, add pepper then stir in
oil.

Divide tomato mixture between 2
bread halves. Reassemble and wrap
firmly in foil. Refrigerate overnight. Cut
into thin slices to serve.
Serves 10-12

HOT-FILLED LOAVES

1 long French loaf
FRENCH ONION BREAD
250 g cream cheese
1 packet French onion soup mix
CHEESE AND CHIVE BREAD
60 g butter
250 g cream cheese
2 tablespoons chopped parsley
2 tablespoons chopped chives
2 tablespoons chopped fresh herbs
freshly ground pepper
GARLIC AND HERB BREAD
3 cloves garlic, crushed
100 g butter
2 tablespoons chopped parsley
pinch mixed herbs
MUSSEL BREAD
105 g can smoked mussels, drained
250 g cream cheese
1 tablespoon chopped parsley
HAM AND BLUE CHEESE BREAD
100 g butter
1 tablespoon chopped parsley
60 g ham, finely minced
30 g blue vein cheese

Combine ingredients of the filling of your
choice. Slice bread and spread slices
with filling. Put the loaf back together
again and wrap in aluminium foil. Bake at
200°C (400°F) for 10 minutes, open the
foil wrapping and bake a further 5-10
minutes until loaf is crisp and cheese is
hot. Serve immediately in bread basket.
Note: Bread sticks can be filled, wrapped
in foil and frozen ready for baking.

WHOLEMEAL NUT BREAD

3 teaspoons dry yeast
2 teaspoons sugar
2 tablespoons warm water
2¼ cups wholemeal flour
1 cup flour
2 teaspoons salt
3 tablespoons wheatgerm
3 tablespoons crushed pecan nuts
30 g butter, melted
300–450 mL lukewarm milk
1 egg, beaten

Combine yeast, sugar and warm water.
Leave in a warm place for a few minutes
to bubble. Sift flours and salt in bowl, stir
in wheatgerm and yeast mixture, pecan
nuts, butter and 200 mL milk. Sprinkle
surface with flour. Cover with plastic
wrap and stand in warm place for 15 minutes.

Combine enough of remaining milk with
flour mixture to form dough. Place on
floured board and knead for 10 minutes.
Place in greased bowl. Cover with plastic
wrap. Stand 30-40 minutes in warm
place until mixture doubles in quantity.
Punch dough down. Divide in half and
knead each into log shape.

Place in 2 greased loaf tins. Cover with
plastic wrap. Allow dough to rise to top of
tin. Preheat oven to 220°C (425°F).
Glaze with beaten egg and bake for 15
minutes; reduce heat to 200°C (400°F)
and continue cooking 30-40 minutes.
Cool on cake rack.
Makes 2 loaves

*Clockwise from bottom left: Hot-filled
Loaves; Patafla; Savoury Scone Roll*

Left to right: Damper; Fruit and Tea Damper

DAMPER

4 cups self-raising flour
1 teaspoon salt
30 g butter
1 cup milk
½ cup water

Sift together flour and salt into a large mixing bowl. Using fingertips gently rub butter to resemble fine breadcrumbs. Make a well in the centre and gradually add combined milk and water mixing with knife to form a soft, slightly sticky dough. Turn dough onto a lightly floured board and knead to form a smooth round shape.

Lightly grease a baking tray or heatproof dish. Place dough on tray and bake at 200°C (400°F) for 25 minutes, then reduce heat to 180°C (350°F) and bake a further 15–20 minutes until the damper sounds hollow when tapped. Serve sliced with butter or jam.
Makes 1 loaf

FRUIT AND TEA DAMPER

½ cup chopped dried apricots
½ cup chopped raisins
¾ cup dried dates, pitted and chopped
finely grated rind 1 orange
2 cups warm tea
60 g butter, softened
1 teaspoon allspice
2 tablespoons sugar
1 quantity damper (see recipe)

Combine fruits in a small bowl, cover with tea and set aside for 30 minutes to soak. Drain very well then combine with butter, allspice and sugar. Pat damper dough out to form a circle approximately 30 cm in diameter. Place fruit in the centre. Fold edges of circle towards centre (the circle should now be a square) and pinch edges together to encase filling.

Carefully place fruit damper on a greased baking tray and brush lightly with a little beaten egg. Bake at 200°C (400°F) for 25 minutes, then reduce heat to 180°C (350°F) and bake a further 15–20 minutes, or until well risen. Cool slightly before serving, otherwise the filling will be too hot.
Makes 1 loaf

Savoury Scone Roll
1 Roll pastry out flat

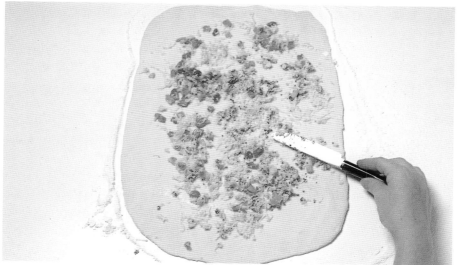

2 Spread filling evenly

3 Roll up pastry

SAVOURY SCONE ROLL

**3 cups self-raising flour
pinch cayenne pepper
1 teaspoon salt
60 g butter
1 cup milk
FILLING
2 rashers bacon, diced and cooked
1 cup grated tasty Cheddar cheese
1 tablespoon French grain mustard
½ teaspoon paprika
1 egg, beaten, to glaze**

Sift flour, cayenne pepper and salt in a large mixing bowl. Rub butter into flour until mixture resembles breadcrumbs. Make a well in the centre and gradually add milk, mixing with a knife to form a soft dough. Turn dough out onto a lightly floured board and knead.

Roll out dough to form a rectangle, 30 x 25 cm. Combine filling ingredients and sprinkle over dough leaving a 2.5 cm border of dough around the edges. Starting at the longest edge, roll up Swiss roll fashion to enclose filling. Place seam side down on baking tray. Lightly brush with beaten egg.

Bake at 200°C (400°F) for approximately 20 minutes or until roll is well risen and golden brown then serve hot.
Serves 6

The Sweetest Treats Imaginable

BRANDY ORANGE SAVARIN

2 cups flour
¼ teaspoon salt
3 teaspoons dry yeast
¾ tablespoon sugar
⅔ cup warm milk
2 eggs, beaten
125 g softened butter
¼ cup glace cherries
2 glace pineapple rings, cut into eighths

SYRUP
⅔ cup water
100 mL orange juice
1 cup sugar
1.5 cm piece vanilla bean
3 tablespoons brandy

GLAZE
½ cup sweet orange marmalade
1 tablespoon water
1 tablespoon orange liqueur (eg
  Curacao *or* Cointreau)

Sift flour and salt together in a bowl. Combine yeast, sugar and warm milk. Make well in flour. Add yeast mixture. Sprinkle over a little flour. Cover with plastic wrap. Allow to rise in a warm place for 15 minutes.

Add eggs and softened butter and mix to a smooth elastic dough. Cover mixture with plastic wrap and again leave in a warm place to double in bulk — 30 minutes.

Place mixture into well-greased 23 cm ring mould or cake tin. Allow to stand, covered with plastic wrap, until mixture rises to top of tin. Bake at 200°C (400°F) for 20 minutes.

Combine ingredients for syrup in saucepan. Stir over heat until sugar dissolves. Bring to boil, boil for 10 minutes, then strain. While Savarin is hot, pour over hot syrup. Allow Savarin to stand 30 minutes until syrup is absorbed. Turn onto serving plate.

To make glaze, combine marmalade, water and orange liqueur in saucepan. Heat for 5 minutes. Glaze Savarin with three-quarters of mixture. Decorate with glace cherries and pineapple pieces. Drizzle over remaining glaze. Serve sliced with whipped cream.
Serves 8

MOCHA CHEESECAKE

CRUST
1 packet semi-sweet chocolate
  biscuits, crushed
1 cup walnuts, crushed
100 g butter, melted

FILLING
450 mL cream, whipped
3 eggs, separated
250 g cream cheese
3 tablespoons sugar
1 tablespoon coffee powder *combined
  with* 1 tablespoon hot water
¼ cup chocolate liqueur
2 teaspoons gelatine
3 tablespoons hot water, extra

GARNISH
150 ml cream
chocolate curls
glace cherries

Combine biscuit crumbs, walnuts and melted butter. Press biscuit mix into base of 23 cm spring-form cake tin. Bake at 190°C (375°F) for 10 minutes then chill.

Whip cream. Cream egg yolks with cream cheese. Blend in sugar, coffee and hot water and chocolate liqueur. Dissolve gelatine in hot water over low heat. Whisk egg whites until stiff. Combine egg whites, cream, cream cheese mixture and gelatine. Blend evenly. Pour cheesecake mixture into tin.

Chill overnight in refrigerator. Remove outside of spring-form tin. Whip extra cream. Pipe rosettes of cream onto top of cheesecake. Decorate with chocolate curls and glace cherries. Return to refrigerator until ready to serve.
Serves 6–8

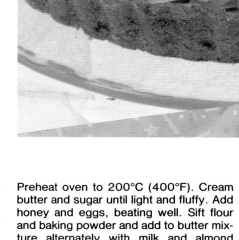

FUDGE CAKE

180 g butter
¾ cup sugar
1 tablespoon honey
3 eggs
2 cups self-raising flour
1 tablespoon baking powder
⅔ cup milk
½ teaspoon almond essence

CREAM FILLING
125 g butter
1½ cups icing sugar
juice ½ lemon

FUDGE ICING
125 g butter
1 tablespoon honey
2 tablespoons milk
2 cups icing sugar
flaked almonds *and* chocolate curls, to
  garnish

Preheat oven to 200°C (400°F). Cream butter and sugar until light and fluffy. Add honey and eggs, beating well. Sift flour and baking powder and add to butter mixture alternately with milk and almond essence.

Divide mixture between 3 x 20 cm greased and lined cake tins. Bake for 18–20 minutes or until cooked when tested. Remove from tins to cake rack and allow to cool.

To make filling, beat butter and icing sugar together with lemon juice. Sandwich cake layers together with cream mixture.

To make Fudge Icing, combine butter, honey and milk in saucepan. Gently heat until butter melts, then heat until nearly boiling. Remove from heat and sift in icing sugar, beating until icing thickens. Spread icing over top of cake and allow to drizzle down the sides. Cool and decorate with almonds and chocolate curls.

Clockwise from left: Mocha Cheesecake; Meringue Baskets; Brandy Orange Savarin

CHOCOLATE LIQUEUR ROLL

125 g cooking chocolate
2 tablespoons strong black coffee
4 eggs, separated
¾ cup caster sugar
2 tablespoons cocoa, sifted
½ cup cream, whipped
1 tablespoon Kirsch
extra ¼ cup cream, whipped
4 strawberries, cut into fans

Melt chocolate in double saucepan with the coffee. Beat egg yolks and sugar until thick. Whisk egg whites until stiff. Fold melted chocolate into egg yolks. Fold in egg whites. Spoon mixture into greased and lined Swiss roll tin. Bake at 210°C (412°F) for 10 minutes. Turn off oven. Leave cake mixture for 15 minutes in oven. Leave cake in tin, cover with damp tea towel till cool. Turn out onto a sheet of greaseproof paper dusted with cocoa. Spread with whipped cream flavoured with Kirsch. Roll up and chill. Decorate with whipped cream rosettes and strawberry fans.
Serves 8–10

PECAN NUT MERINGUES

3 egg whites
pinch cream of tartar
1 cup caster sugar
⅔ cup chopped pecan nuts
20 crushed salty crackers
1 teaspoon vanilla
1 teaspoon cornflour
extra pecan nuts
½ cup cream, whipped

Whisk egg whites with cream of tartar until stiff. Gradually add sugar. Beat until stiff. Fold in chopped pecans, crushed crackers and vanilla.

Lightly dust oven tray with cornflour. Pile mixture onto tray, spread out to 5 cm circles. Bake at 150°C (300°F) for 30 minutes. Transfer to serving plate. Allow to cool and decorate with nuts and whipped cream.
Serves 6–8

45

PARTY COCKTAIL TRIFLE

25 g packet red jelly crystals
2 cups boiling water
1 large jam-filled Swiss roll
3 tablespoons sherry
600 mL milk
2 eggs
2 tablespoons cornflour
vanilla essence
2 tablespoons sugar
300 mL cream, whipped
2 tablespoons desiccated coconut, toasted

Combine jelly crystals and boiling water until dissolved. Pour into shallow baking tin. Allow to set in refrigerator then cut up roughly. Slice Swiss roll into 1.5 cm slices. Line base and sides of glass serving dish with cake slices. Sprinkle sherry over cake slices.

In large saucepan combine milk, eggs, cornflour, vanilla and sugar and whisk till fluffy. Bring to boil whisking until thickened. Allow to cool slightly. Pour over cake slices. Chill overnight. Top with jelly and pipe with cream to decorate. Sprinkle with toasted coconut before serving.
Serves 6–8

BLACK FOREST CREPE CAKE

CREPE MIXTURE
pinch salt
2 cups flour
2 eggs
600 mL milk
20 g butter
FILLING
440 g can pitted black cherries
¼ cup orange-flavoured liqueur
2 tablespoons sugar
2 tablespoons cornflour
GARNISH
1 cup cream, whipped
3 tablespoons almond flakes, toasted

Sift salt and flour together; blend in eggs and milk to form a smooth batter.

Grease crepe pan with butter. Pour 1 tablespoon crepe mix into hot pan, turn pan to cover base thinly with mixture. Cook until dry on surface. Continue until 15–20 crepes have been made. Layer crepes between paper towel and allow to cool.

Place cherries, liqueur, sugar and cornflour in saucepan. Bring to boil, stirring. Allow to thicken and then cool. Mould crepes together with cherry filling.

Spreading filling between each layer. Form crepes into dome shape.

Whip cream. Coat outside of crepes with cream. Pipe crown of rosettes on top of cake. Decorate sides of cake with toasted almonds. Refrigerate until serving. Serve sliced.
Note: Keeps 1–2 days in refrigerator.
Serves 10–12

MERINGUE BASKETS

2 egg whites
½ cup caster sugar
¼ teaspoon cream of tartar

Whisk egg whites until stiff. Add sugar beating well for 20 minutes. Fold in cream of tartar. Fit piping bag with large rose pipe. Fill with egg white mixture and pipe meringue in small 10 cm rounds forming a basket shape on lightly oiled tray.

Bake at 110°C (225°F) until crisp but still white. Baking time can vary from 2–4 hours. Allow to cool in oven. Fill baskets with whipped cream and fruit and serve.
Makes 8

CHOCOLATE MERINGUE BASKETS
Add 2 teaspoons sieved cocoa

COFFEE MERINGUE BASKETS
Add 2 teaspoons instant coffee powder

Left to right: Meringue Baskets; Party Cocktail Trifle; Mocha Cheesecake

Black Forest Crepe Cake

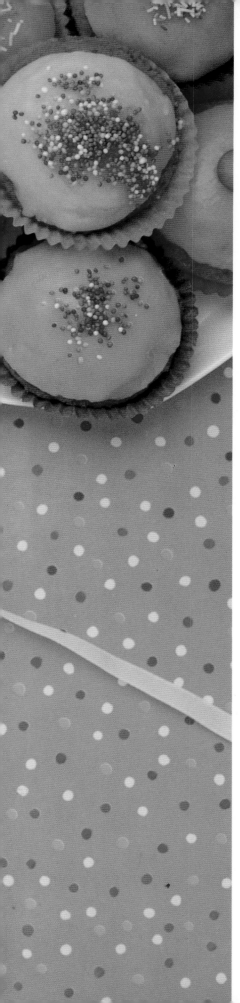

Children's Birthday Parties

Sugar and spice and all things nice: that's what children's birthday parties are made of. The excitement which builds over the weeks is almost unmanageable by The Day. This chapter of savoury and sweet recipes brings together ideas for parties for toddlers through to the more sophisticated palates of young teenagers.

Savoury Beginnings

TRAFFIC LIGHTS

24 slices brown bread
60 g butter
4 processed cheese slices
4 small tomatoes, sliced
6 lettuce leaves, shredded
salt and pepper, to taste
¼ cup shredded carrot

Spread bread slices lightly with butter. Cut crusts from bread. Using a round 1.5 cm biscuit cutter, press 6 holes into 12 of the bread slices. Cut each slice of processed cheese into thirds. Using remaining 12 slices of bread, arrange layers of tomato, cheese and lettuce to form traffic light colours, then top with salt, pepper and carrot. Top with cut-out slices of bread. Cut each sandwich in half.
Makes 24

RIBBON SANDWICHES

4 slices white bread
4 slices brown bread
softened butter
3–6 different sandwich fillings (see recipe)

Remove crusts from bread. Thinly butter bread. Spread 1 of the fillings on a slice of white bread. Top with slice of brown bread. Spread with second filling. Continue layering bread, using alternate slices of white and brown bread and spreading with filling. Cut sandwich in half, then each half into 4, making ribbon layer sandwiches.
Makes 8

PINWHEELS

1 loaf unsliced white bread
softened butter
3–6 different sandwich fillings (see recipe)

Remove crusts from loaf of bread. Cut bread in half. Carefully slice each half into 8 slices lengthways. Thinly butter each slice and spread evenly with filling. Roll up each slice lengthways and secure each roll with toothpick. Continue with remaining bread and filling.
Makes 8

SANDWICH FILLINGS

☆ Meat *or* seafood paste
☆ Salmon
☆ Cream cheese mixed with finely chopped dried fruits/walnuts/chives/celery/finely grated lemon and carrot
☆ Finely mashed egg with mayonnaise
☆ Chopped lettuce and ham
☆ Cheese spread *or* herbed processed cheese
☆ Mashed sardines
☆ Chicken and celery mixed with mayonnaise
☆ Peanut butter and sultanas
☆ Peanut butter and honey
☆ Peanut butter and finely shredded lettuce
☆ Mashed banana, lemon juice and desiccated coconut

Children's party cakes

HOT TUNA BREAD

1 French bread stick
225 g can tuna, drained
1 small onion, chopped
1 stick celery, chopped
2 tablespoons mayonnaise
1 tablespoon chopped parsley
1 teaspoon lemon juice
pepper, to taste
3 slices processed cheese

Preheat oven to 180°C (350°F). Halve bread lengthways and scoop out bread from crust. Mix together tuna, onion, celery, mayonnaise, parsley, lemon juice and pepper. Spoon tuna mixture into bread case.

Halve cheese slices diagonally. Layer cheese over top of tuna. Cover with top of bread stick. Wrap in foil and bake for 25 minutes. Five minutes before serving, open foil so that cheese will melt and bread will crust. Serve in slices.
Serves 6

PIZZA

2 cups flour
pinch salt
3 teaspoons dry yeast
½ teaspoon sugar
⅔ cup warm milk
2 tablespoons olive oil
TOPPING
4 tomatoes, sliced
2 onions, sliced and separated into rings
250 g salami, sliced
1 teaspoon mixed herbs
60 g mozzarella cheese, grated
1 tablespoon chopped parsley
2 tablespoons olive oil
OPTIONAL EXTRAS
¼ cup chopped olives
½ cup sliced mushrooms
½ cup cooked peeled prawns

Sift flour and salt into a bowl. Combine yeast, sugar, warm milk and olive oil. Cover and leave in a warm place for 5 minutes or until bubbly.

Make a well in centre of flour, pour in milk mixture. Sprinkle with flour, cover with plastic wrap and leave in a warm place for 15 minutes until yeast mixture bubbles again.

Work mixture to form dough. Knead dough on floured board for 10 minutes or until smooth and elastic. Halve and roll out each piece to a 20 cm circle; for smaller pizzas, roll each piece of dough into 5 x 8 cm rounds. Place on greased baking trays.

Divide topping ingredients between pizzas. Place layer tomato slices on base, add onion rings, salami, mixed herbs and mozzarella cheese. Top with parsley and sprinkle with olive oil. Allow pizzas to stand for 15 minutes. Preheat oven to 200°C (400°F). Bake for 40 minutes and serve hot.
Note: Sprinkle any of the extras over the salami layer. Pizza bases, wrapped well in plastic, may be frozen for up to 6 months.
Makes 2 x 20 cm pizzas or 10 x 8 cm pizzas

CHINESE SPRING ROLLS

1 tablespoon oil
1 onion, finely chopped
125 g lean ham, diced
125 g bean sprouts
1 teaspoon soy sauce
oil, for deep-frying
8 spring roll wrappers

Heat oil in wok and stir-fry onions until transparent. Add ham and bean sprouts, stir-fry gently for 1½ minutes. Stir soy sauce through mixture. Allow to cool.

Spoon 2 tablespoons ham and onion filling on to each spring roll wrapper, fold over at ends and roll up, pressing edges in firmly. Stand for 15 minutes.

Heat oil in wok. Deep-fry spring rolls until golden. Serve hot with dipping sauce.
Serves 4

BACON-WRAPPED BEEF AND APPLE BURGERS

750 g minced lean beef
⅓ cup breadcrumbs
¼ cup finely chopped onion
1½ teaspoons Worcestershire sauce
pepper, to taste
2 apples, grated
6 bacon rashers

Combine beef, breadcrumbs, onion, Worcestershire sauce, pepper and apple in a bowl. Form mixture into 6 patties. Wrap a bacon rasher round each burger securing with toothpick. Grill burgers for 10 minutes, turning once to brown each side. Serve on hamburger bun with salad and sauce.
Serves 6

SAY CHEESE PIES

2 cups flour
pinch cayenne pepper
90 g butter
1 cup grated tasty cheese
2–3 tablespoons iced water
milk, to glaze
FILLING
1 large onion, sliced
30 g butter
2 hard-boiled eggs, peeled and chopped
180 g Cheddar cheese, diced
1 tablespoon chopped parsley
½ teaspoon nutmeg
pepper, to taste

Sift flour and cayenne into a bowl. Rub through butter till mixture resembles fine breadcrumbs. Add cheese and water to form dough.

Knead lightly on floured board. Roll out dough to 6 mm thickness. Cut into 16 rounds to fit patty tins. Press 8 rounds into base of patty tins. Prick base lightly. Set aside. Preheat oven to 220°C (425°F).

Saute onion in butter until transparent, drain. Combine onion with remaining filling ingredients and divide filling between pastry-lined patty tins. Damp edges of pastry, cover with remaining pastry rounds. Seal edges together. Make small hole in centre of top of each pie. Brush with milk. Bake for 30 minutes then remove from tins to rack. Serve hot or cold.
Makes 8

Pizzas (above) and Pinwheel Sandwiches (below)

SESAME DRUMSTICKS

8 chicken drumsticks
¼ cup seasoned flour
1 egg, beaten
3 tablespoons sesame seeds
¼ cup toasted breadcrumbs
60 g butter, melted

Wipe drumsticks, dip in seasoned flour, then beaten egg and coat in combined sesame seeds and breadcrumbs.

Place drumsticks on greased baking tray and bake at 180°C (350°F) for 30 minutes. Brush drumsticks with butter. Continue cooking a further 15–20 minutes or until golden brown. Serve hot or cold.
Makes 8

SAVOURY EGG BOATS

6 hard-boiled eggs
210 g can tuna, drained
½ cup finely chopped celery
¼ cup mayonnaise
pepper, to taste
¼ teaspoon dry mustard
3 slices bread
finely chopped parsley, to garnish

Peel and halve eggs lengthways. Remove yolk from white and mash yolk finely. Combine mashed yolks with tuna, celery, mayonnaise, pepper and mustard and pile into egg white halves. Cut crusts off bread. Cut each piece of toast into 4 triangles. Insert 1 triangle on top of each stuffed egg boat to resemble a sail. Garnish with chopped parsley. Refrigerate until serving time.
Makes 12

BUSH BABY SALAD

2 cups alfalfa sprouts
2 celery stalks
½ cup raisins
120 g cherry tomatoes, halved
4 carrots, peeled and cut into matchsticks
1 cup corn kernels

Spread alfalfa sprouts over a large serving plate. Cut celery into 6 cm lengths and arrange attractively on the alfalfa with the remaining ingredients.
Serves 6

SAUSAGE AND BACON PLAIT

1 packet frozen ready-rolled puff pastry, thawed
1 egg, beaten
1 tablespoon sesame seeds
FILLING
350 g minced pork
150 g bacon, chopped
1 onion, chopped
1 tablespoon chopped parsley
salt and pepper, to taste
¼ teaspoon mixed herbs

Roll out pastry to 25 cm square on a lightly floured surface. Combine filling ingredients and place along centre of pastry. Cut pastry on each side of filling into diagonal strips 1.5 cm wide. Brush with beaten egg.

Place strips from each side alternately over the sausage mixture to form a plait. Place plait onto lightly greased baking tray, glaze with egg, sprinkle with sesame seeds and bake at 200°C (400°F) for 30–40 minutes or until cooked. Serve hot.
Serves 6

TUNA AND NOODLE BAKE

¾ cup macaroni, cooked
220 g can tuna, drained
⅓ cup mayonnaise
½ cup chopped celery
salt and pepper, to taste
130 g can condensed cream of celery soup
⅓ cup milk
100 g grated tasty cheese
¼ cup breadcrumbs
1 tablespoon chopped parsley, to garnish

Combine macaroni, tuna, mayonnaise, celery, salt and pepper. Blend together soup and milk over heat, stirring until heated through, but do not boil. Add half the cheese, stir until melted.

Fold soup mixture with macaroni and noodle mixture. Place into 2 litre casserole dish. Sprinkle with remaining cheese and breadcrumbs. Bake at 180°C (350°F) for 20 minutes. When cooked, sprinkle with parsley to serve.
Serves 6

MEATBALL BOATS

500 g minced meat
1 cup grated tasty cheese
2 tablespoons tomato sauce
pepper, to taste
½ cup desiccated coconut
15 cheese slices
30 thin slices cucumber

Combine minced meat, cheese, tomato sauce and pepper. Form mixture into 30 meatballs. Toss in coconut until well coated. Place on greased oven tray and bake at 200°C (400°F) for 15 minutes.

Cut each cheese slice into 2 triangles. Place 1 cheese slice and 1 cucumber slice together. Secure through top and bottom with toothpick to form the mast and sail. Attach to the meatball. Serve meatballs hot or cold.
Makes 30

SPICY CHICKEN PIECES

1 cup soy sauce
½ cup vegetable oil
3 teaspoons grated ginger root
½ cup chicken stock
2 teaspoons Chinese five-spice powder
2 tablespoons honey
1.5 kg chicken pieces

Combine first 6 ingredients in a small saucepan and heat until simmering. Remove from heat. Pat chicken pieces dry with paper towel and place in a large dish. Pour over soy sauce mixture, cover and refrigerate for at least 6 hours.

Lift chicken pieces from marinade and arrange in baking dish and bake at 180°C (350°F) for 30 minutes, basting occasionally with remaining marinade. To test if chicken is cooked, pierce flesh with a skewer. The juices should run clear without any signs of pink. Serve hot or cold.
Note: If serving chicken at a barbecue, cook over moderately hot coals turning frequently.
Serves 10

Clockwise from top left: Sausage and Bacon Plait; Bush Baby Salad; Sesame Drumsticks; Savoury Egg Boats

COCKTAIL BANANA KEBABS

6 cocktail frankfurts
2 bananas, peeled
3 bacon rashers
6 x 2.5 cm pieces pineapple
6 button mushrooms

Thread cocktail frankfurts onto skewers. Cut each banana into thirds. Add piece banana to skewer. Cut bacon rashers in half. Roll each half and secure onto skewer. Finish with piece of pineapple then mushroom.

Place under preheated grill and cook until all sides are browned. Serve hot.
Serves 6

KIWI FRUIT AND NUT SALAD

1 lettuce
4 kiwi fruit, peeled and sliced
2 oranges, peeled and segmented
4 radishes, thinly sliced
100 g button mushrooms, thinly sliced
small cucumber, thinly sliced
1 stick celery, thinly sliced
50 g cashew nuts
¼ cup French dressing
shredded orange peel, to garnish

Tear lettuce into pieces. Mix all ingredients together in salad bowl and toss with dressing. Alternatively, dressing may be served separately. Garnish with fine shreds of orange peel.
Serves 4–6

WATERMELON SALAD

½ watermelon
1–2 rock melons
3 cups cooked rice
440 g can whole corn kernels
500 g black grapes, peeled and seeded
500 g white grapes, peeled and seeded
mint or basil leaves, to garnish

Remove watermelon seeds. Scoop all flesh out of melons using a melon baller. Combine ingredients and pile into watermelon shell. Cover with foil or plastic wrap and chill. Serve garnished with mint or basil leaves. Vinaigrette dressing *(see recipe)* can be poured over salad if desired.
Serves 6–8

Sweet Treats

TOFFEE APPLES

10 red apples
TOFFEE
250 g butter
1 cup sugar
3 tablespoons water
¼ teaspoon salt
1 teaspoon vanilla

Remove stalks from apples and push a wooden skewer into each one.

Place toffee ingredients in saucepan and heat until sugar dissolves, stirring occasionally. Bring to boil. Boil rapidly, without stirring, until the toffee reaches 145°C (280°F) or until a spoonful of mixture, when dropped in cold water, separates into threads which are hard but not brittle. Carefully dip apples into toffee one at a time. Cover apple completely. Plunge into ice water for 5 seconds. Stand on well-oiled greaseproof paper until set.
Makes 10

ALPHABET BISCUITS

125 g butter
½ cup caster sugar
2 cups flour
¼ teaspoon baking powder
2 egg yolks
1 teaspoon vanilla essence
1 teaspoon grated lemon rind
pinch salt
hundreds and thousands
chocolate vermicelli
¼ cup chopped glace cherries
ICING
1 cup icing sugar
2–3 tablespoons lemon juice

Preheat oven to 200°F (400°F). Cream butter and sugar. Fold in flour, baking powder, egg yolks, vanilla essence, lemon rind and salt to form a stiff dough. Wrap dough in plastic wrap and refrigerate 1 hour.

Roll out dough to 30 cm square. Cut into 26 x 1.5 cm blocks. Roll into sausage shapes 1.5 cm in diameter, form into the 26 alphabet letters and flatten slightly. Place on greased baking tray and bake for 8–10 minutes. Allow to cool on tray 2 minutes before removing to cake rack.

Stir icing sugar with lemon juice to give a thick icing. Ice letters while still warm. Decorate with hundreds and thousands, chocolate vermicelli or glace cherries. Allow to cool and set.
Makes 26

POPCORN BALLS

3½ cups uncooked popping corn
140 g butter
1½ cups molasses
¼ cup water
½ cup sugar
1 tablespoon vinegar
½ teaspoon salt
1 tablespoon vanilla
OPTIONAL ADDITIONS
1 cup desiccated coconut
1 cup raisins
1 cup salted peanuts
1 cup puffed wheat

Place popping corn and 60 g butter in large saucepan. Cover with lid. Allow butter to melt, then shake pan, holding lid on, over heat to pop corn. Continue shaking until popping stops. Turn corn into warm large bowl. Stir in any optional additions at this point.

In saucepan combine molasses, water, sugar, vinegar and salt. Cook over medium heat, stirring occasionally, until mixture heats to 135°C (275°F) or a small amount dropped into ice water separates into hard but not brittle threads.

Remove from heat and add 80 g butter and vanilla. Gradually pour hot syrup into the centre of the popped corn. Quickly stir corn and syrup to coat.

With buttered hands, gather and press corn into firm balls. Push wooden skewer into ball. Allow to cool. Wrap each ball in a square piece of cellophane, drawing the paper around the ball and twisting on top.
Makes 15

Clockwise from top: Emerald Smoothie; Patty Cakes; Toffee Apples; Popcorn; Alphabet Biscuits

VICTORIA SANDWICH

Delicious as a simple sponge or decorated as a birthday cake, this is a very useful basic recipe.

125 g butter
½ cup caster sugar
2 eggs
1 cup self-raising flour
3 tablespoons jam
icing sugar

Preheat oven to 175°C (340°F). Cream butter and sugar until soft. Whisk eggs, beat into sugar mixture. Fold in flour. Spoon mixture into 2 greased and lined 15 cm sponge tins. Bake for 20 minutes. Remove cakes from tins and cool on cake rack.

Spread jam onto first cake and sandwich to second. Sprinkle top with icing sugar or ice and decorate as a birthday cake.

SERVING SUGGESTIONS

Try decorating your cake with some of the following: flowers, small toys, marzipan miniature fruits, smarties, jaffas or other sweets, hundreds and thousands, glace fruits, silver balls, whipped cream, sliced fresh fruit, candles and anything else that appeals to your imagination. Boys or athletic girls may like a cricket cake: use green icing for grass, desiccated coconut for the pitch, candles for stumps, a jaffa for a ball and small dolls to represent players. Girls may like heart-shaped cakes with plenty of fancy icing decorations. Try using different shaped tins — there is plenty of variety available.

JELLY CAKES

1 quantity Victoria Sandwich (see recipe)
2 × 25 g packets raspberry jelly crystals
2 cups boiling water
2 cups desiccated coconut
300 mL thickened cream, whipped

Make Victoria Sandwich according to directions. Lightly grease 2 patty tins. Place 1–2 tablespoons of cake mixture into patty tins and bake in the top half of the oven at 180°C (350°F) for 15–20 minutes or until well risen and golden brown. Turn out onto a cake rack to cool.

Dissolve jelly in boiling water and pour into a heatproof dish deep enough to cover a cake. Place in refrigerator and allow to partially set. The jelly should resemble the consistency of egg white. Sprinkle coconut on a large sheet of greaseproof paper. Dip each cake in jelly then roll in coconut to coat. If a thicker coating is desired, repeat process.

Place jelly cakes in a single layer on a tray and refrigerate until set. One or 2 hours before serving, cut a little off the top of each cake. Place a small spoonful of cream on each cake and replace their tops before serving.
Makes approximately 30

Cricket Cake (see Victoria Sandwich)
with Jelly Cakes

THE GINGERBREAD LOG CABIN

1 kg thick honey
1 cup water
5 cups rye flour
3½ cups wholemeal flour
1 cup chopped mixed peel
1 teaspoon ginger
1 teaspoon cinnamon
½ teaspoon nutmeg
1 teaspoon bicarbonate of soda

ICING
2 egg whites
3 cups icing sugar
1 tablespoon lemon juice

DECORATION
glace cherries
blanched almonds
sweets
plastic toy trees *and* people

Bring honey and water to boil in a saucepan, stirring continuously. Leave to cool.

Sift flours and add mixed peel, spices and bicarbonate. Make well in centre and add honey mixture. Blend mixture into a soft dough. Refrigerate dough wrapped in plastic wrap overnight.

Divide dough into 6 equal portions. If dough is too stiff set aside in a warm place for 15 minutes until easy to handle.

To make roof, roll out 2 portions to 6 mm thickness and 20 cm square. Set aside on lightly greased tray and prick with a fork.

To make walls, use 3 portions of dough and roll into sausage shapes about 1 cm in diameter.

The 4 walls require a total of:
28 logs 20 cm long
4 logs 19 cm long
2 logs 16.5 cm long
2 logs 12.5 cm long
2 logs 10 cm long

To make each end wall, place on lightly greased tray side by side:
7 x 20 cm logs
1 x 19 cm log
1 x 16.5 cm log
1 x 14 cm log
1 x 12.5 cm log
1 x 10 cm log

To make remaining 2 walls, place on a greased tray side by side:
7 x 20 cm logs
1 x 19 cm log

Preheat oven to 200°C (400°F). Bake roof 12–18 minutes then cool on cake rack. Leaving 2 mm gap between each log, bake each wall 12–18 minutes. During baking, the gaps close to form the wall. Allow to cool on rack.

From 1 wall cut out:
1 door 2.5 x 6.5 cm
1 window 4 x 2.5 cm

With remaining dough, make:
4 logs 2.5 cm long and 1.2 cm thick

On baking tray place 2 logs next to each other and 2 logs on top to make double layer — this forms the chimney.

Knead remaining uncooked dough. Roll into flat 6 mm thick square 22 x 22 cm. This will form the base of the house. Prick with fork. Place on tray with chimney logs and bake 12–18 minutes. Cool on cake rack.

Whisk egg whites and fold in icing sugar to form smooth paste. Add lemon juice.

Place base on board. Using icing, join 4 walls together at corners on top of base. Allow to dry completely at each stage of construction. Join roof to house with icing.

Thin 3 tablespoons of icing with a few drops of water. Gently drizzle icing over roof to resemble snow. Attach chimney to roof.

Divide window cut out in half. Place each half on either side of window to resemble shutters and attach with icing. Decorate house and garden with icing, cherries, nuts, sweets and plastic toys. Allow to set completely.

1   *Make 2 walls and 2 end walls*
2   *Join walls*
3   *Join roof to house with icing*
4   *Drizzle icing over roof to make snow*

1

2

3

4

The Gingerbread Log Cabin

PATTY CAKE PARADE

1 quantity Victoria Sandwich batter
  (*see recipe*)
GLACE ICING
1½ cups pure icing sugar, sifted
5 g butter
1–2 tablespoons boiling water
few drops food colourings of your
  choice

Line 2 patty cake trays with paper cups and fill two-thirds full with spoonfuls of Victoria Sandwich mixture. Bake at 180°C (350°F) for 15–20 minutes or until cakes are well risen and golden brown. Turn out onto a wire rack to cool before icing.

To make icing, combine icing sugar and butter in a bowl and beat; gradually add enough boiling water to mix. Add colourings, leaving 1 bowl of icing white. Ice cakes and decorate imaginatively: use white icing to pipe names of party guests or rosettes onto iced cakes; garnish with hundreds and thousands, chocolate vermicelli, silver balls, glace cherries, jellybabies, smarties or other favourite sweets. Let your imagination create a colourful variety where every cake is different — they look wonderful massed together on large trays or serving platters.

Note: To achieve a smooth finish on your icing, use a round bladed knife and dip from time to time in hot water. Uniced cakes can· be made in advance and frozen.
Makes 24

CHOCOLATE BUTTERFLY CAKES

125 g butter
½ cup caster sugar
2 eggs, beaten
¾ cup self-raising flour
¼ cup cocoa
1 tablespoon warm water
chocolate vermicelli, to sprinkle
150 mL cream, whipped

Preheat oven to 190°C (375°F). Cream butter and sugar till smooth. Beat in eggs. Fold in sifted flour and cocoa alternately with water. Beat mixture 2 minutes. Spoon mixture into 20 paper-lined patty tins. Bake for 15 minutes. Cool on a cake rack.

Cut tops off cakes and halve. Spoon 1–2 teaspoonfuls of cream on top of each cake and press in the tops to form wings. Sprinkle each butterfly with chocolate vermicelli.
Makes 20

SUPERB CHOCOLATE CAKE

2 cups flour
⅔ cup caster sugar
⅓ cup cocoa
1 tablespoon baking powder
1 teaspoon bicarbonate of soda
pinch salt
1 cup milk
125 g butter *or* margarine, melted
2 eggs

Preheat oven to 190°C (375°F). Grease and line a 20 cm deep cake tin.

Sift dry ingredients twice in a bowl. Combine milk and butter and add to dry ingredients. Beat with an electric mixer for 2 minutes. Add eggs and beat again for 2 minutes.

Bake in a preheated moderately hot oven for 50–60 minutes or until cooked when tested. Remove and cool on a cake rack. Ice with chocolate icing and decorate as desired.

ALMOND CHOCOLATE FUDGE

360 g cooking chocolate
400 g can condensed milk
2 teaspoons vanilla
1 cup roasted almonds, chopped

Melt chocolate in top of double saucepan. Blend in condensed milk, stirring until combined. Remove from heat. Add vanilla and beat until smooth. Fold in almonds. Pour mixture into greased square cake tin. Chill in refrigerator until set. When firm, cut into 2.5 cm squares.
Makes 40 squares

NOUGAT WALNUT SPONGE

SPONGE
12 eggs, separated
1 cup sugar
3 cups self-raising flour
½ teaspoon bicarbonate of soda
pinch salt
FILLING
100 g nougat
¼ cup apricot conserve
60 g butter
3 tablespoons sugar
1 tablespoon boiling water
1 tablespoon milk
¼ teaspoon vanilla
1 cup crushed walnuts
220 g can peach slices, drained
¼ cup glace cherries
¼ cup water
2 teaspoons sugar
2 teaspoons gelatine

Blend egg yolks and sugar together. Sift flour, bicarbonate and salt together. Whisk egg whites till stiff. Fold egg yolks, flour mixture and egg whites together.

Grease and line the base of a 23–25 cm spring-form cake tin. Place one-third of cake mix into tin. Bake at 180°C (350°F) for 10–15 minutes or until lightly browned. Remove from tin immediately. Remove paper from base, allow to cool. Repeat with second and third layers of cake mix.

Place 1 layer on serving plate. Melt nougat in a double saucepan and spread over cake base. Spread thin layer apricot conserve over nougat. Add second layer. Cream butter and sugar till smooth and sugar is dissolved. Gradually blend in boiling water. Beat 2 minutes. Fold in walnuts. Spread walnut cream over cake layer.

Add remaining cake layer. Decorate with peach slices. Place cherries, water, sugar and gelatine in saucepan. Bring to boil; boil 2 minutes. Cool slightly, spoon over top of cake and allow to set. Serve sliced.
Note: Refrigerate no more than 3 days.
Serves 12–16

RAINBOW CAKE

250 g butter
1 teaspoon vanilla
1 cup sugar
4 eggs
2½ cups self-raising flour
1 cup flour
¾ cup milk
1 drop red food colouring
60 g chocolate, melted

FILLING
⅓ cup raspberry jam
300 mL cream, whipped

VANILLA ICING
125 g white chocolate
2 cups icing sugar
⅔ cup milk
250 g butter
1 teaspoon vanilla

Preheat oven to 200°C (400°F). Cream butter, vanilla and sugar. Add eggs, one at a time and beat well. Sift flours and fold in alternately with milk. Divide mixture evenly into three. Leave one third plain, colour one third pink with red food colouring, and add melted chocolate to remaining third.

Spoon different coloured mixtures in alternating rows into a greased and lined cake tin (see step by step). Bake for 20–25 minutes. Cool on cake rack. When cold, remove paper lining, sandwich layers together with raspberry jam and whipped cream, and ice with vanilla icing.

Melt chocolate in top of double saucepan. Blend together icing sugar, milk, butter and vanilla, fold in melted chocolate. Allow to set and decorate as desired.

Rainbow Cake

1 Divide cake mixture between three bowls

2 Leave one bowl plain and colour one pink

3 Add melted chocolate to third bowl

4 Place mixture in alternating rows using two-thirds of tin

5 Add a final row of mixture along one side of tin

FROZEN FRUIT POPSICLES

2 cups strawberries, washed
½ cup concentrated apple juice
½ cup unsweetened pineapple juice

Place strawberries in a food processor or blender and process until smooth. Add remaining ingredients and process a further 30 seconds. Transfer mixture into a jug and pour into ice block moulds. Place in freezer and freeze for at least 6 hours.
Makes 12

ORANGE BOMBS

12 large oranges
2 litres vanilla ice cream
¾ cup orange juice concentrate, well
** chilled**
finely grated rind 1 orange
few drops orange food colouring
orange leaves or blossom, to garnish
** (optional)**

Cut top third from each orange. Using a small knife, loosen orange flesh from just inside skin. Carefully scoop down into the oranges and remove as much flesh and membrane as possible. Reserve orange flesh for fruit juice.

Remove ice cream from freezer and allow to soften slightly. Place in large mixing bowl and, using a metal spoon, stir in remaining ingredients. If ice cream starts to soften too much, return to freezer for a few minutes.

Place orange shells on baking trays. Spoon ice cream into shells until almost full (the filling will expand when frozen). Place in freezer for 2 hours then remove and wrap in plastic wrap. Return to freezer then place bombs in refrigerator for 30 minutes before serving. The ice cream filling will soften slightly and the orange shells will collect a frosty 'bloom'. Serve topped with orange leaves or blossom if in season.
Makes 12

Left to right: Frozen Fruit Popsicles and Orange Bombs

Diet Delights

These days, everyone is aware of the importance of their health and well-being. At a time when more people enjoy international cuisine, no one wants to subsist on carrot sticks and shrivelled lettuce. The following recipes from around the world offer delicious, attractive and health-conscious party dishes.

Delicious Soups

CHILLED LEEK AND POTATO SOUP

4 leeks
20 g polyunsaturated margarine *or* unsalted butter
1 kg potatoes, peeled and sliced
2 litres homemade Chicken Stock (*see recipe*)
freshly ground pepper, to taste
250 g low-fat yoghurt
¼ bunch chives, chopped

Remove darker green leaves from leeks. Halve leeks lengthways almost to the root end. Wash well, separating leaves to clean. Drain, cut off root end and slice.

Heat margarine, add leeks, cover pan and cook for 5 minutes. Add potatoes, and stock and pepper. Bring to boil, reduce heat and simmer for 20–30 minutes until potato is tender. Set aside to cool.

Drain soup, reserving cooking liquid. Puree cooked vegetables in batches, adding reserved liquid as necessary. Combine puree and remaining cooking liquid and adjust seasoning. About 1 hour before serving, add yoghurt. Serve soup chilled, sprinkled with chives.
Serves 10–12

CREAMY CARROT SOUP

2 teaspoons polyunsaturated oil *or* margarine
1 onion, finely chopped
1 clove garlic, crushed
1 kg carrots, peeled and chopped
1 litre Chicken Stock (*see recipe*)
freshly ground pepper, to taste
1 cup low-fat yoghurt
1 teaspoon cornflour
3–4 tablespoons chopped parsley
2 tablespoons chopped chives, to garnish

Heat oil in pan, add onion and garlic and saute 5 minutes, stirring occasionally. Add carrots, chicken stock and pepper and bring to boil. Reduce heat and simmer, partially covered, for about 20 minutes until carrot is tender. Cool for a few minutes.

Puree soup, return to rinsed pan and reheat soup gently. Add some hot soup to combined yoghurt mixture and cornflour mixture and stir well. Add yoghurt mixture to soup and heat, stirring.

Just before serving, add parsley. Pour soup into a heated tureen and serve garnished with chives.
Serves 10–12

Salad Greens with Tomato Dressing and Fruit

GAZPACHO

1 kg tomatoes, peeled, seeded and
    chopped
½ cucumber, seeded and diced
3–4 cloves garlic, finely chopped
4 shallots, finely sliced
½ green capsicum, diced
2 tablespoons oil, olive or
    polyunsaturated
1–2 tablespoons white wine vinegar
salt (optional)
freshly ground pepper, to taste
Tabasco sauce, to taste
3 tablespoons chopped parsley
2½ cups iced water

GARNISH
½ cucumber, seeded and diced
½ green capsicum, diced
3 slices wholemeal bread, diced

Combine tomatoes, cucumber, garlic,
shallots, capsicum, oil and vinegar with
salt, pepper, Tabasco sauce and parsley;
chill well. Just before serving stir through
iced water.

Serve soup in chilled bowls. Place
cucumber, capsicum and bread in small
bowls. Guests can help themselves to
garnish as liked.
Note: For those people permitted it, 2
eggs, hard-boiled, can be chopped and
offered as another garnish.
Serves 10–12

HERBED YOGHURT AND CUCUMBER SOUP

1 litre low-fat yoghurt
500 mL chicken stock (see recipe)
chopped garlic, to taste
2 cucumbers
100 g pecans, very finely chopped
1–2 tablespoons oil, olive or
    polyunsaturated
1–2 tablespoons chopped mint
1 tablespoon chopped dill
freshly ground pepper, to taste

Place yoghurt in a bowl and beat well. Stir
through chicken stock and garlic and chill
in refrigerator.

If cucumber has a thick skin, peel it,
otherwise leave the skin on. Halve the
cucumbers lengthways and scoop out
seeds. Dice cucumber flesh. Stir cucumber into yoghurt mixture with remaining
ingredients. Serve chilled.
Serves 10-12

CHICKEN STOCK

1 kg chicken backs or stock pieces
water, to cover
1 onion, studded with 3 cloves
few celery leaves
1 carrot, roughly chopped
bouquet garni
½ teaspoon whole black peppercorns

Wash chicken, discard skin and trim off
fat. Place bones in a pan with water to
cover and bring to boil, skimming as
necessary. Add remaining ingredients,
reduce heat and simmer partially
covered, for 1½–2 hours. Skim as
necessary.

Strain stock and allow to cool. Chill
overnight and remove any fat that has
risen to the surface. Use stock as
directed.
To store: Refrigerate for up to 1 week,
simmering every 2–3 days. Alternatively
freeze in usable quantities. 250 mL (1
cup) quantities are a useful size. It is
always handy to have frozen cubes of
chicken stock, so another useful method
is to freeze 2 ice-cube trays of stock.
Place frozen cubes into a plastic bag,
seal and label.
Makes approximately 4 cups

International Smorgasbord

MUSSELS AND SNOW PEAS

1 kg mussels
250 g snow peas, trimmed
10–12 fresh lychees, peeled
4 slices ginger root, finely sliced
½ cup Tomato Dressing (see recipe)

Scrub mussels and pull out beard. Discard any mussels with broken or open
shells. Bring 1 cup water to boil, add
mussels, cover and steam for 3–5 minutes until they open. Remove mussels
from shells and place in a bowl. Cover
and set aside.

Cover snow peas with boiling water
and leave for 1 minute. Drain and cool
with water. Add snow peas to mussels.
Halve lychees and remove stones. Place
with mussels. Sprinkle ginger over.

Pour dressing over mussel mixture and
stir to coat all ingredients. Cover and chill
for 30 minutes. Drain off any excess
dressing. Serve on individual plates.
Serves 10–12

FISH WITH HERBED YOGHURT DRESSING

16 fish fillets
few parsley stalks
few celery leaves
1 teaspoon black peppercorns
bouquet garni
½ cup dry white wine
2 cups water
double quantity Herbed Yoghurt
    Dressing (see recipe)

Check fish fillets for bones and set aside.
Combine parsley, celery, peppercorns,
bouquet garni, wine and water in frying
pan. Bring to boil, reduce heat and simmer for 5 minutes.

Pour dressing into a heatproof container and stand in a bowl of very hot
water. Stir occasionally so dressing heats
through.

Simmer fish fillets in cooking liquid for
3–5 minutes until cooked when tested
(cooking time depends on thickness of
fillets). Drain fish and arrange on a serving plate. Spoon dressing over and
serve.
Serves 10–12

*Clockwise from top left: Mussels and
Snow Peas; Gazpacho; Herbed Yoghurt
and Cucumber Soup*

BAKED SNAPPER

2 x 2 kg whole snapper, scaled and
    cleaned
2 lemons
freshly ground pepper, to taste
6 shallots, finely chopped
1 stalk celery, finely chopped
2 teaspoons polyunsaturated oil
4 cups wholemeal fresh breadcrumbs
grated rind 1 orange
juice 2 oranges
salt (optional)
few sprigs fennel
extra 2 lemons

Grate rind of 1 lemon and set aside.
Squeeze lemons and brush juice over
skin and inside cavity of both fish.
Season cavity with pepper and set aside
for 30 minutes.

Heat oil and fry shallots and celery 3
minutes. Drain off any oil. Combine
breadcrumbs with vegetables, lemon and
orange rind and enough orange juice to
bind ingredients. Taste and adjust
seasoning. Stuff fish with filling and
secure with skewers. Place sprigs of fennel on top.

Place fish in greased baking dishes,
cover with greased foil and bake at
180°C (350°F) for 40–60 minutes until
cooked when tested.

Remove foil and fennel and arrange
fish on serving platters. Garnish with
extra fennel and lemon wedges. Serve
with steamed seasonal vegetables and
salad.
Serves 10–12

BEEF AND BROCCOLI
WITH SOY SAUCE
DRESSING

750 g broccoli, cut in florets and
    blanched
500 g lean roast beef, sliced thinly
1 red capsicum, seeded and sliced
125 g mushrooms, sliced
1 cup bean sprouts
230 g can water chestnuts, drained
    and halved
freshly ground pepper, to taste
¼ cup white wine vinegar
¼ cup soy sauce
1 teaspoon grated ginger root
1 tablespoon vegetable oil

In a large salad bowl combine broccoli,
beef, capsicum, mushrooms, bean
sprouts and water chestnuts; season well
with pepper. Combine remaining ingredients and pour over salad just before serving.
Serves 6

LAMB AND
VEGETABLE KEBABS

2 kg boned leg of lamb
1½ cups Tomato Dressing (see recipe)
300 g button mushrooms
3 green capsicums, seeded

Trim lamb of all visible fat. Cut meat into
3 cm cubes and place in a bowl with
Tomato Dressing; leave to marinate a
minimum of 4 hours. Soak wooden
skewers in water to cover for at least 30
minutes. Remove meat from the marinade
and reserve liquid. Trim mushroom stalks
and cut capsicums into pieces the same
size as the lamb. Thread lamb, mushrooms and capsicums alternately onto
drained skewers.

Grill kebabs 12–15 minutes until
cooked as liked. During cooking, turn
kebabs and brush with reserved liquid.
Serves 10–12

SPINACH ROLLS

4 dried Chinese mushrooms soaked in
    water 10 minutes
2 teaspoons oil
1 shallot, chopped
1 clove garlic, crushed
1 teaspoon ginger
1 cup shredded cabbage
½ cup chopped celery
½ cup grated carrot
1 cup bean sprouts
¼ cup chopped water chestnuts
2 tablespoons soy sauce
1 tablespoon sesame oil
1 tablespoon dry sherry
2 tablespoons cornflour
salt and pepper, to taste
1 bunch spinach

Remove mushroom stalks, drain and
slice. Heat oil, stir-fry mushrooms, shallot
and garlic 3 minutes. Add ginger, cabbage, celery, carrot, bean sprouts and
water chestnuts. Cook 5 minutes. Combine soy sauce, sesame oil and sherry;
blend in cornflour and stir into vegetables. Adjust seasoning and cook mixture until it thickens and boils. Allow to
cool.

Wash spinach and remove hard stems.
If large, cut spinach leaves into shapes
about 12 cm square. If small, use whole
spinach leaves. Place 1 tablespoon of
mixture on each spinach leaf, roll up and
seal ends. Steam rolls over boiling water
until spinach is tender. Serve hot.
Serves 4

FRENCH ROAST
CHICKEN

2 x 1.4 kg chickens
10 g polyunsaturated margarine
2 tablespoons water
250 g button mushrooms, chopped
4 tablespoons chopped parsley
5 cups fresh wholemeal breadcrumbs
salt (optional)
freshly ground pepper, to taste
juice 2 lemons
1 litre Chicken Stock (see recipe)

Rinse and wipe chickens, discard fat
found in body cavity, neck and giblets.

In a frying pan simmer margarine,
water and mushrooms for 5 minutes.
Allow excess liquid to evaporate and set
aside to cool.

Combine mushrooms, parsley, breadcrumbs, salt and pepper. Divide stuffing
between both chickens. Truss chickens
for roasting and preheat oven to 190°C
(375°F).

Boil chicken stock in 2 roasting dishes
on top of stove. Put a rack in each dish
and arrange chickens, on their sides, on
the racks. Brush chickens with lemon
juice and cover with foil.

Roast for 20 minutes. Turn chickens
onto their other side, brush with more
lemon juice, cover with foil again and
roast a further 20 minutes.

Turn chickens onto their backs, brush
with lemon juice and roast, covered, for
a further 20 minutes. Remove foil and
continue roasting, basting occasionally,
until cooked through. Turn oven off and
let chickens stand for 5 minutes before
carving.
Serves 10–12

Baked Snapper; French Roast Chicken

Slimline Salads

SALAD GREENS WITH TOMATO DRESSING

1 cos lettuce, washed
1 butter lettuce, washed
4 shallots, trimmed and sliced
1 green capsicum, sliced
2 tablespoons chopped parsley
4–6 tablespoons Tomato Dressing (see recipe)

Tear both lettuces into pieces. Place in a salad bowl with shallots, capsicum and parsley. Toss lightly. Cover and chill until serving time. Just before serving, add dressing and toss to coat all the ingredients.
Serves 10–12

TOMATO AND CAPSICUM SALAD

750 g tomatoes, peeled
1 bunch shallots, thinly sliced
3 green capsicums, sliced
⅓ cup Salad Dressing (see recipe)
⅓ cup Herbed Yoghurt Dressing (see recipe)

Cut tomatoes into wedges, discarding core section. Place in a bowl with shallots and capsicums. Mix dressings together and stir into salad. Serve chilled.
Serves 10–12

FENNEL AND ORANGE SALAD

3 heads fennel
3 oranges
4–6 tablespoons Tomato Dressing (see recipe)
2 tablespoons chopped parsley

Trim fennel, slice thinly; wash well and discard any discoloured slices. Cut both ends from oranges then cut off all rind and pith. With a small sharp knife, cut between membranes of oranges and free segments. Remove any seeds. Combine oranges, fennel and dressing. Cover, chill and serve sprinkled with parsley.
Serves 10–12

CAULIFLOWER AND BROCCOLI SALAD

500 g cauliflower
500 g broccoli
1 cup Creamy Vinaigrette Dressing (see recipe)
1–2 teaspoons French mustard
1 teaspoon capers, chopped
Tabasco sauce, to taste
paprika, to taste

Wash cauliflower and broccoli and separate into florets. Cook broccoli and cauliflower separately until tender but still crisp. Drain and cool. Combine dressing with mustard, capers and Tabasco sauce. Adjust seasonings to taste. Arrange cooked vegetables in a serving dish and spoon dressing over. Cover and chill until serving. Serve sprinkled with paprika.
Serves 10–12

BROWN RICE SALAD WITH TOMATO DRESSING

2 oranges, segmented
2 cups brown rice, cooked
4 shallots, sliced
1 large red capsicum, diced
1 large green capsicum, diced
1 cup Tomato Dressing (see recipe)
salt (optional)
freshly ground pepper, to taste

Cut rind and all pith from oranges. With a small sharp knife, cut between the membrane and flesh of each segment and free the orange flesh. Remove and discard any seeds.
   Combine oranges, rice, shallots and capsicums. Pour dressing over and toss lightly. Season to taste. Place in a serving bowl, cover and chill until serving time.
Serves 10–12

Clockwise from top: Tomato and Capsicum Salad; Salad Greens with Tomato Dressing; Cauliflower and Broccoli Salad

Dressing up

SALAD DRESSING

2 tablespoons cornflour
⅔ cup reduced fat milk
1 tablespoon prepared mustard
1 tablespoon margarine
1 egg, beaten
2 tablespoons vinegar
⅓ cup polyunsaturated oil
salt (optional)
freshly ground pepper, to taste

Mix cornflour with a little milk. Heat remaining milk to simmering. Add corn-flour mixture, stir well and simmer until thickened. Remove from heat and stir in mustard and margarine. Beat in egg, then gradually add vinegar and oil. Return mix-ture to pan and heat gently until thick, stirring constantly. Do not allow to boil. Allow dressing to cool. Add seasonings. Use as directed.
Makes approximately 1¼ cups

HERBED YOGHURT DRESSING

1 cup low-fat yoghurt
2 tablespoons chopped parsley
1 tablespoon chopped chives
1 tablespoon prepared mustard
salt (optional)
freshly ground pepper, to taste

Combine yoghurt, herbs and seasonings in a bowl. Store in an airtight container and refrigerate before using. Use as directed.
Makes approximately 1 cup

FRENCH DRESSING

¼ cup white wine vinegar
salt and freshly ground pepper, to taste
½ teaspoon sugar
½ teaspoon mustard powder
1 clove garlic, peeled and lightly pressed
½ cup olive oil

Combine vinegar, salt and pepper, sugar, mustard and garlic in a screw-topped jar or blender. Shake or process until well blended. Gradually add oil and mix until combined.
Makes ¾ cup

Left to right: Salad Dressing; Herbed Yoghurt Dressing; French Dressing; Tomato Dressing; Creamy Vinaigrette Dressing

TOMATO DRESSING

1 cup tomato juice
juice 1 lime *or* ½ lemon
2 shallots, finely chopped
2 cloves garlic, chopped
Worcestershire sauce, to taste
Tabasco sauce, to taste
freshly ground pepper, to taste

Combine all ingredients and mix thoroughly. Store in an airtight container in the refrigerator. Use as directed.
Makes 1 cup

CREAMY VINAIGRETTE DRESSING

This recipe is the basis of many fine salad dressings that add pizzazz to leafy green vegetables. To vary the flavour or add a gourmet touch, use the unique flavours of walnut, almond, or rape oil blended with a little herb or strawberry vinegar. These are all quite strong, so use sparingly and combine with vegetable oil or white vinegar to make the correct proportions.

½ cup white wine vinegar
salt and freshly ground pepper
1 cup olive oil (or a combination of ½ olive oil and vegetable oil)

Combine all ingredients in a screw-topped jar and shake.
Makes 1½ cups

Unforbidden Fruits

ORANGE SORBET

10 oranges
1 tablespoon gelatine
2 tablespoons water
½ cup water extra
sugar substitute, to taste
4 egg whites

Squeeze juice from oranges and strain. Sprinkle gelatine over water and leave for a few minutes. Place container of gelatine in hot water and stir until dissolved. Combine with orange juice and add sweetening to taste.

Pour mixture into a cake tin and freeze until half-frozen. Tip mixture into a bowl and beat well to break down ice-crystals. Place in refrigerator.

Whisk egg whites until stiff and fold into orange juice mixture. Return mixture to freezer and freeze until half-frozen. Turn into a bowl again and beat to break down ice crystals. Refreeze. Beat once more if liked.
Note: If you own an ice cream maker, follow the manufacturer's instructions.
Serves 10–12

CHILLED LEMON SOUFFLE

375 mL can evaporated skimmed milk
2 tablespoons gelatine
4 tablespoons water
pinch salt (optional)
grated rind and juice 4 lemons
powdered or liquid sweetener, to taste
4 kiwi fruit, peeled and sliced

Chill evaporated milk in refrigerator for 24 hours. Sprinkle gelatine over water and leave to stand for a few minutes. Place container of gelatine in hot water and stir until dissolved then set aside.

In a large chilled bowl, whisk milk and salt until frothy. Beat in gelatine, lemon rind, juice and sweetener. The dessert should taste lemony — add more juice and rind if necessary. Pour into a serving bowl and refrigerate to set. To serve, arrange kiwi fruit decoratively on top of souffle.
Serves 10–12

SUMMER FRUIT PLATTER

Fresh fruits are a good choice for dessert being low in fat and salt and high in fibre. During the summer months we are lucky to have a wide variety of reasonably priced fruits available to choose from. Tropical fruits only can be selected, stone fruits only or a mixture of both. Remember to select fruit that is free from bruises and soft spots. Wash all edible skinned fruit before preparing.

TROPICAL
1 large ripe pineapple
1 ripe pawpaw
3 ripe mangoes
10–12 lychees (optional)
STONE FRUITS
10–12 ripe apricots
10–12 ripe plums
10–12 ripe peaches
250–500 g cherries
MIXED FRUITS
2 punnets ripe strawberries
6 kiwi fruit
1 rock melon
500 g seedless grapes

Tropical selection: Top and tail pineapple. With a sharp knife cut off skin, including all eyes. Halve pineapple lengthways. Cut each half into 6 wedges then cut off core. Halve and seed pawpaw and cut into 12 wedges. Cut mango on each side of stone. Set aside stone section. Cut the flesh on the other sections into diamond shapes. Peel lychees. Arrange fruit on a platter. Cover and chill until serving time.

Stone Fruits: Halve apricots, plums and peaches and remove stones. Arrange all fruits on a platter. Cover and chill until serving time.

Mixed Fruits: Hull strawberries. Peel kiwi fruit and quarter. Halve rock melon, remove seeds and cut into 12 wedges. Cut fruit from rind. Separate grapes into bunches. Arrange fruit on a platter. Cover and chill until serving time.
Each selection serves 10–12

MELON SALAD

1 rock melon
1 honeydew melon
½ watermelon
¼ bunch mint, shredded

Halve rock melon and honeydew melon and scoop out seeds. Cut flesh into balls or pieces using a melon baller or knife. Remove as many seeds from watermelon as possible. Cut flesh into balls or pieces.

Place all melon pieces in a serving bowl. Sprinkle mint over and stir. Cover and chill until serving time.

VARIATION
Substitute fresh ginger for mint. Cut 6–8 slices peeled ginger into strips and stir through melon.
Serves 10–12

STRAWBERRY SNOW

3 punnets ripe strawberries
sugar substitute, to taste
2 tablespoons gelatine
4 tablespoons water
6 egg whites

Wash and hull strawberries, puree and sweeten to taste. Sprinkle gelatine over water and leave to stand for 5 minutes. Place container of gelatine in hot water to dissolve then stir gelatine into strawberry puree.

Whisk egg whites to form stiff peaks; fold into strawberries. Taste and adjust for sweetness. Spoon strawberry snow into a serving bowl, cover and chill until serving time.
Serves 10–12

RHUBARB FOOL

2 bunches rhubarb
sugar substitute, to taste
2½ cups skim milk
5 tablespoons custard powder

Trim rhubarb and cut into 5 cm pieces. Wash and place in a pan with enough water to cover half-way. Bring to boil, reduce heat and simmer, covered, until tender. Drain, reserving liquid. Puree fruit, adding liquid as necessary and sweeten to taste.

Place most of the milk in a pan. Combine remaining milk with custard powder and stir into milk. Bring to boil, stirring, and simmer until thick. Cool slightly. Mix custard and rhubarb, taste and adjust for sweetening. Spoon into a serving bowl. Cover and chill until serving time.
Serves 10–12

Clockwise from top: Strawberry Snow; Orange Sorbet; Chilled Lemon Souffle

Teatime

One of the most civilised of rituals, afternoon tea or a late-night supper gives us all the chance to get together with friends and family. The following recipes offer both traditional and innovative treats to satisfy every sweet tooth.

CUSTARD VANILLA SQUARES

375 g ready-rolled frozen puff pastry, thawed
CUSTARD
4 cups milk
⅔ cup sugar
60 g butter
1 cup cornflour
1 teaspoon gelatine
1 tablespoon hot water
2 egg yolks, beaten
2 teaspoons vanilla
ICING
200 g icing sugar, sifted
1 tablespoon water
2 tablespoons passionfruit pulp

Preheat oven to 220°C (425°F). Roll out pastry to 60 x 30 cm rectangle. Cut in half widthways. Place on 2 baking trays, sprinkle with cold water and prick with fork. Stand pastry for 10 minutes then bake 12–18 minutes. Allow to cool on cake rack.

Combine 3 cups milk with sugar and butter in a pan. Dissolve sugar over low heat, stirring, then bring to boil. Blend remaining milk with cornflour. Dissolve gelatine in hot water and add to cornflour mixture. Add cornflour mixture to hot milk and heat, stirring until thick and smooth. Remove from heat and beat in egg yolks and vanilla. Allow to cool.

Blend icing sugar, water and passionfruit pulp. Trim pastry layers to fit Swiss roll tin. Spread icing over 1 layer of pastry and allow to set. Place second layer of pastry on bottom of Swiss roll tin. Spread with very cool custard mixture. Top with iced pastry layer. Allow to set for 20 minutes before cutting into 5 cm squares to serve.
Makes 32

Clockwise from left: Austrian Cherry Walnut Cake; Apricot Banana Bread; Lemon Cheese Tartlets; Citrus Ring Biscuits; Caramel Chelsea Bun

COCONUT PLUM FINGERS

BASE
¾ cup wholemeal flour
¾ cup self-raising flour
125 g butter
¼ cup caster sugar
vanilla, to taste
1 egg
¼ cup milk
TOPPING
½ cup plum conserve
1 cup chopped raisins
1 egg
2 tablespoons sugar
1¼ cups coconut

Preheat oven to 220°C (425°F). Sift flours together twice. Cream butter and sugar together. Blend in vanilla and egg. Fold in flour mixture and milk alternately. Press mixture evenly into greased 30 x 25 cm lamington tin. Spread with plum conserve and sprinkle with raisins. Combine egg, sugar and coconut. Spread carefully over top of raisins.

Bake for 10 minutes then reduce heat to 180°C (350°F) for further 10–15 minutes. Allow to cool in tin 10 minutes before cutting into 5 x 2.5 cm fingers. Allow to cool a further 5 minutes before removing from tin to cake rack to cool completely. Store in airtight container.
Makes 24

COFFEE CREAM

1 quantity Victoria Sandwich mixture
  (*see recipe*)
2 tablespoons cornflour
2 tablespoons caster sugar
2 tablespoons instant coffee powder
1¼ cups milk
250 g butter
2 tablespoons icing sugar
2 tablespoons flaked almonds
glace cherries

Preheat oven to 220°C (425°F). Prepare Victoria Sandwich mixture. Spread mixture evenly into greased and lined Swiss roll tin. Bake for 10–12 minutes.

Turn cake out onto greaseproof paper and remove lining paper. Leave to cool, then cut into 3 even strips lengthways.

Blend cornflour, sugar and coffee with 2 tablespoons milk. Heat remaining milk, stir in cornflour mixture and return to heat. Bring to boil, stirring until thickened. Place a piece of wet greaseproof paper or plastic wrap on the surface of 'sauce' and leave to cool.

Cream butter and icing sugar. Beat gradually into coffee sauce. Spread mixture over 2 of the cake layers, then sandwich together. Cover top and sides with coffee cream and sprinkle with flaked almonds. Decorate with piped rosettes of coffee cream and glace cherries.

AUSTRIAN CHERRY WALNUT CAKE

1 cup glace cherries
2¼ cups self-raising flour
185 g butter
⅔ cup caster sugar
3 eggs
¾ cup milk
1½ cups walnuts, finely chopped
½ cup desiccated coconut

Grease and line a 23 cm square cake tin. Preheat oven to 180°C (350°F). Halve the cherries and mix with 4 tablespoons of flour.

Beat butter until soft. Add sugar and continue beating until mixture is light and fluffy. Add eggs, one at a time, beating well between additions.

Fold in flour and milk alternately, starting and finishing with flour. Fold in cherries, walnuts and coconut.

Spoon mixture into prepared tin and bake for 50–60 minutes until cooked when tested. Remove and cool on a cake rack.
Makes 16–20 pieces

HAZELNUT SHORTBREAD

250 g butter
⅓ cup caster sugar
90 g ground hazelnuts
1⅔ cups flour
100 g chocolate
30 g extra ground hazelnuts

Preheat oven to 180°C (350°F). Beat butter and sugar until creamy. Mix in hazelnuts and sifted flour. Put mixture into piping bag with fluted tube and pipe rounds into base of greased patty tins. Bake for 15 minutes. Remove from patty tins to cake rack to cool. Melt chocolate in bowl placed over hot water and stir. Dip shortbread half-way into chocolate. Place on aluminium foil to set. Sprinkle chocolate with extra ground hazelnut. Store in airtight container.
Makes 25

CARAWAY SEED CAKE

2 cups flour
2 teaspoons nutmeg
1 teaspoon bicarbonate of soda
1 teaspoon baking powder
125 g butter
1 teaspoon vanilla
1 cup caster sugar
½ cup brown sugar
3 eggs
1 teaspoon caraway seeds
½ cup sour milk
TOPPING
4 tablespoons sugar
1½ teaspoons cinnamon
2 teaspoons grated orange rind
¾ cup soft breadcrumbs
40 g butter, melted

Preheat oven to 200°C (400°F). Sift flour, nutmeg, bicarbonate and baking powder twice. Cream butter, vanilla and sugars until light and fluffy. Beat in eggs. Fold in flour mixture and caraway seeds, alternately with sour milk. Place mixture into a 20 cm greased and lined cake tin.

To make topping, combine all ingredients and sprinkle over top of cake. Bake for 20–25 minutes or until cooked. Cool on cake rack and serve.

Left to right: Coffee Cream and Caraway Seed Cake

CARAMEL CHELSEA BUN

150 g butter
½ cup brown sugar
¼ cup chopped walnuts
½ cup chopped glace cherries
3½ cups self-raising flour
½ teaspoon salt
2 eggs, beaten
1¼ cups milk
30 g extra butter, melted
½ cup sugar
2 teaspoons cinnamon
1 cup raisins, finely chopped

Preheat oven to 220°C (425°F). Cream 60 g butter and all the brown sugar. Spread over base of a 23 cm square cake tin. Sprinkle with walnuts and cherries and set aside.

Sift flour and salt. Rub in remaining butter to resemble breadcrumbs. Combine eggs and milk. Add to flour mixture to form soft dough. Knead dough lightly on floured board. Roll out to rectangle shape, 6 mm thick.

Brush surface with melted butter. Sprinkle with sugar, cinnamon and raisins. Roll up dough from longest side to form log shape. Cut into 2.5 cm pieces. Place cut side down into tin. Bake 25-30 minutes until cooked. Invert onto plate to cool. Serve sliced.

APRICOT BANANA BREAD

1 cup chopped dried apricots
¼ cup sherry
1¼ cups flour
2 teaspoons baking powder
½ teaspoon bicarbonate of soda
¼ teaspoon salt
90 g butter
grated rind 1 lemon
⅔ cup caster sugar
2 eggs
½ cup mashed banana

Preheat oven to 180°C (350°F). Soak apricots in sherry for 1 hour. Drain and discard sherry. Sift flour, baking powder, bicarbonate of soda and salt twice. Cream butter, lemon rind and sugar. Beat in eggs one at a time. Fold in fruits alternately with flour mixture. Place mixture into a greased and lined loaf tin. Bake for 1 hour or until cooked. Cool on cake rack. Ice if desired, with icing of your choice.

Clockwise from left: Apricot Banana Bread; Caramel Chelsea Bun; Citrus Ring Biscuits

CITRUS RING BISCUITS

1 cup flour
¼ teaspoon allspice
150 g butter
½ cup caster sugar
1 egg
grated rind 1 lemon
1 cup ground almonds
2 cups soft breadcrumbs
1 egg yolk, beaten
ICING
200 g icing sugar, sifted
2 tablespoons lemon juice
60 g candied orange and lemon rind

Preheat oven to 200°C (400°F). Sift flour and spice together twice. Cream butter and sugar. Beat in egg and lemon rind. Fold in ground almonds and breadcrumbs to form dough. Wrap dough in plastic wrap and chill for 1 hour.

Divide dough into 30 pieces and roll each piece until 10 cm long. Brush ends with egg yolk and join together to form ring. Place on greased baking trays. Bake 10-15 minutes. Remove to cake rack to cool.

Combine icing sugar and lemon juice. Ice biscuits and decorate with strips of candied rind.
Makes 30

ALMOND SWEETMEATS

250 g ground almonds
125 g icing sugar
4-6 tablespoons orange-blossom water
125 g pistachio nuts, peeled and finely chopped
1½ tablespoons caster sugar
extra 125 g icing sugar
extra 125 g pistachio nuts, peeled

Combine ground almonds and icing sugar with enough orange-blossom water to form a stiff paste. Knead until smooth and allow to rest. Shape paste into small walnut-sized balls.

Using a teaspoon handle, make a small hole in each ball and fill it with combined pistachio nuts and caster sugar. Close hole over filling and reshape. Roll balls in icing sugar and place in small paper cups. Decorate the top of each ball with a peeled pistachio nut. Serve with coffee.
Note: To peel pistachio nuts, simmer for 3 minutes, drain and slip off skins. Dry on a paper towel before use.
Makes about 40

STRAWBERRY JELLY ROLLS

1 packet red jelly crystals
1½ cups boiling water
1 cup desiccated coconut
SPONGE
4 eggs, separated
2 egg yolks extra
grated rind 1 lemon
½ cup caster sugar
4 tablespoons flour
1 tablespoon cornflour
FILLING
60 g butter
3 tablespoons sugar
1 tablespoon boiling water
1 tablespoon milk
vanilla, to taste
1 cup chopped strawberries

Dissolve jelly crystals in boiling water by stirring well. Refrigerate to cool but not set. Preheat oven to 220°C (425°F).

Whisk egg yolks, lemon rind and half the sugar till creamy. Whisk egg whites till stiff, add remaining sugar and fold into egg yolk mixture. Sift flour and cornflour and fold into egg mixture.

Spread evenly in a greased and lined Swiss roll tin. Bake for 10-12 minutes or until cooked. Remove from oven and cover with a damp tea towel until cold.

To make filling, cream butter and sugar for 5 minutes. Gradually add boiling water, milk and vanilla, beating thoroughly. Stir through strawberries.

Turn cake out and remove lining paper. Spread with strawberry cream, cut into 12 squares and roll each one up. Dip into cold jelly, roll in coconut and place on greaseproof paper to set.
Makes 12

PINE NUT MACAROONS

2 cups sugar
3 cups ground almonds
1 teaspoon vanilla essence
4 egg whites
1 cup pine nuts

In a food processor place sugar, ground almonds, vanilla and egg whites. Whirl for a minute or so, to form a smooth paste. Mix whole pine nuts into this mixture and with the help of a spoon form walnut-sized balls and place on greased biscuit tray. Bake at 160°C (325°F) for 10-12 minutes.
Serves 4-6

LEMON CHEESE TARTLETS

PASTRY
1 cup flour
pinch salt
90 g butter
squeeze lemon juice
1 egg yolk
FILLING
½ cup sugar
2 tablespoons cornflour
2 tablespoons flour
⅔ cup water
2 egg yolks
grated rind 1 lemon
40 g butter
⅓ cup lemon juice

Preheat oven to 230°C (450°F). Sift flour
and salt in a bowl. Rub in butter. Add
lemon juice and egg yolk to form dough.
Knead on lightly floured board. Roll out
dough to 3 mm thickness. Cut with fluted
scone cutter into 5 cm rounds.

Line patty tins with pastry rounds.
Prick base and sides of pastry shells.
Bake for 8–10 minutes. Cool on cake
rack. Cut pastry strips from remaining
dough, twist and bake on tray for 6–8
minutes.

To make filling, combine sugar, cornflour, flour and water. Stir over low heat
until mixture simmers and thickens.
Remove from heat. Add yolks, lemon
rind, butter and lemon juice. Set aside to
cool. Spoon lemon cheese mixture into
tartlet cases. Decorate with pastry twist.
Allow to cool completely to serve.
Substitute lemon cheese filling with raspberry jam or caramel-butterscotch filling.

CARAMEL-BUTTERSCOTCH
1 cup brown sugar
⅓ cup flour
3 tablespoons cornflour
pinch salt
4 egg yolks
2¼ cups milk
60 g butter
2 teaspoons vanilla
3 tablespoons golden syrup

Combine brown sugar, flour, cornflour,
salt in a pan. Beat egg yolks and milk
together and add to pan. Beat mixture till
smooth. Gently heat, stirring until mixture
thickens. Remove from heat. Beat in butter, vanilla and golden syrup. Allow to
cool. Use as desired.
Makes 18

*Left to right: Lemon Cheese Tartlets and
Chocolate Nut Slice*

PETITS FOURS

2 quantities Victoria Sandwich (see recipe)
FILLING
1¾ cups apricot jam
250 g almond paste
ICING
1½ cups icing sugar
1–2 tablespoons water
1 tablespoon rum
food colouring
DECORATIONS
glace cherries
chocolate vermicelli
candied coffee beans
crystallised violets
chopped pistachios
silver confectionery balls

Prepare 2 quantities Victoria Sandwich (see recipe) and divide between 3 greased and lined Swiss roll tins. Bake at 220°C (425°F) for 10–12 minutes.

Remove cakes from tins while still warm. Turn out onto clean greaseproof paper, removing paper lining. Carefully halve each cake lengthways, giving 6 layers. Spread each layer of cake with apricot jam. Layer cake together.

Roll out almond paste to the size of the cake. Place on top of cake. Cover with foil or greaseproof paper, weight down with a heavy wooden board and leave for 24 hours. Cut the cake into 3.5 cm squares or shapes.

Beat icing sugar with water and rum till smooth. Colour icing as desired. Coat cake squares in icing. Place on cake rack to dry. Pipe decorations with remaining icing and decorate with cherries, vermicelli etc. When dry, place each square in paper cases to serve.
Makes 28

CHERRY AND NUT STRUDEL

12 sheets filo pastry
100 g butter, melted
1 kg pitted cherries, morello style
¾ cup dried breadcrumbs
1 cup sugar
¼ cup chopped almonds
icing sugar

Preheat oven to 200°C (400°F).

Place filo pastry between 2 dry tea towels and cover with a just damp tea towel to prevent pastry from drying out while cooking. Remove 1 sheet pastry at a time and brush with melted butter. Cover with a second sheet pastry and

brush again with butter. Continue with remaining pastry, using up half the butter.

Combine cherries, breadcrumbs, sugar and almonds. Place on pastry lengthways leaving 2 cm edge. Fold long edge over filling then over sides. Brush with butter. Roll up pastry, brushing with butter to seal ends. Place seam side down onto baking tray. Bake for 30 minutes until browned. Remove from tray to serving plate. Dust with icing sugar to serve.
Serves 8

CHOCOLATE NUT SLICE

125 g butter
½ cup brown sugar
1 tablespoon golden syrup
2 tablespoons cocoa
1 egg, beaten
½ teaspoon vanilla
250 g plain sweet biscuits, crushed
½ cup chopped nuts (walnuts, almonds or pecans)
2 tablespoons desiccated coconut
ICING
90 g chocolate
3 tablespoons water
1 teaspoon oil
2 cups icing sugar, sifted
¼ cup finely chopped nuts (walnuts, almonds or pecans)

Combine butter, sugar, golden syrup and cocoa in saucepan. Stir over low heat to dissolve sugar, then heat until bubbling. Remove from heat and add beaten egg and vanilla, stirring until thick. Add crushed biscuits, nuts and coconut and mix well. Press mixture into greased 28 × 18 cm lamington tin. Chill until firm.

To make icing, combine chocolate, water and oil in a bowl. Place over hot water to melt. Add icing sugar and stir well to combine. Spread chocolate icing over slice. Sprinkle with nuts. Allow icing to set before cutting into squares or fingers to serve.
Makes approximately 20

MELTING MOMENTS

100 g butter, softened
⅓ cup caster sugar
1 egg yolk
few drops vanilla essence
grated rind ½ lemon
1¼ cups self-raising flour, sifted
BUTTERCREAM FILLING
125 g butter, softened
¼ cup icing sugar, sifted
grated rind ½ orange
few drops orange food colouring

Cream butter until light and fluffy. Add caster sugar and beat until dissolved. Beat in egg yolk, vanilla essence and lemon rind. Fold in sifted flour gradually to form a stiff dough. Divide dough into 20 walnut-sized balls.

Place biscuit balls on greased baking tray, flattening slightly to allow for spreading. Bake at 190°C (375°F) for 15 minutes. Cool on a wire rack before sandwiching biscuits together with butter cream.

To make filling, cream butter, add icing sugar and beat until smooth. Add grated rind and food colouring. Spread cream on flat side of 10 biscuits and sandwich together with remaining biscuits.
Makes 20

Melting Moments

Party Drinks for All

Cocktails, punches, whips and fizzy fruit drinks should keep your party bubbling happily for hours. This section gives a variety of delicious beverages for parties of all types and for all ages.

Non-alcoholic Drinks

MULBERRY FRUIT CUP

500 g ripe mulberries
1 cup sugar
2 litres water
juice 1 lemon
strip lemon rind
sherry (optional)

Boil all ingredients except sherry together for 20 minutes. Strain and chill thoroughly. Serve with 1 teaspoon sherry per glass, if liked, and ice cubes.
Makes 2.5 lites

PASSIONFRUIT PUNCH

½ cup sugar
½ cup water
1 cup orange juice
1 cup lemon juice
1 cup passionfruit pulp
ice cubes
750 mL bottle ginger ale *or* passiona
orange and lemon slices for garnish

Bring sugar and water to boil, stirring constantly. Continue to cook for 5 minutes then allow to cool. Add orange and lemon juices and passionfruit. Chill until needed. To serve, place a quantity of ice cubes in punch bowl, pour syrup over ice, pour in ginger ale and garnish with orange and lemon slices.
Makes 1.5 litres

Strawberry Juice and Chilled Fruit Punch

LEMONADE

½ cup lemon juice
¼ cup apple juice concentrate
orange essence, to taste
ice blocks
soda *or* mineral water

Combine lemon juice, apple juice concentrate and orange essence. To 2 tablespoons of mixture, add ice blocks and soda water to fill a glass.
Serves 5–6

PINEAPPLE NECTAR

1 large ripe pineapple

Peel, core and chop pineapple. In a processor, puree until smooth. Strain through fine sieve, pressing down well on pulp with back of spoon. Sealed in a jar this will keep up to 7 days in refrigerator.
Makes 3 cups

MANGO AND COCONUT DELIGHT

2 mangoes, peeled, seeded and
**   roughly chopped**
1 cup coconut milk
1 large lemon, juiced
½ lemon, finely grated
1 tablespoon honey or to taste
1 teaspoon vanilla essence
1 cup crushed ice
GARNISH
6 slices lemon, sliced thinly
mint sprigs

Combine all ingredients and process for 20–30 seconds until smooth and creamy. Pour into tall chilled glasses. To serve, garnish with lemon and mint.
Serves 6

PARTY PUNCH

2 tablespoons tea
2½ cups boiling water
grated rind and juice 3 oranges
grated rind and juice 3 lemons
1 cup sugar
1 cup water
1 cup fruit cordial
pulp 6 passionfruit
1 orange, thinly sliced
1 lemon, thinly sliced
1 lime, thinly sliced
mint sprigs
ice cubes
1 litre bottle ginger ale
1 litre bottle soda water

Make tea with boiling water; infuse for 5 minutes then strain and cool. Simmer grated orange and lemon rinds with sugar and water for 5 minutes. Strain into tea. Add cordial and passionfruit, then chill until needed. Empty into punch bowl, add remaining ingredients and serve.
Makes 3 litres

WATERMELON PINEAPPLE PUNCH

1.5 kg piece watermelon, peeled, seeded and chopped
1¼ cups pineapple juice
1 cup lime juice
1 cup vodka
sugar, to taste
1–2 limes, thinly sliced, to garnish

Puree watermelon in blender or food processor. Force through a fine sieve, discarding any remaining pulp. Stir in pineapple and lime juices and vodka. Add sugar to taste. Chill well and serve garnished with lime slices.
Makes 1.5 litres

STRAWBERRY SODA WHIZZ

2 cups pineapple juice
2 cups ginger ale
2 cups soda water
500 g frozen strawberries
1 cup lemon juice

Combine pineapple juice, ginger ale and soda water. Add strawberries (which will thaw in punch) and lemon juice. Serve chilled with cocktail umbrellas and coloured straws in tall glasses.
Makes 1.5 litres

TROPICAL SUPERWHIP

1 avocado, chopped
1 banana, chopped
¼ cup chopped pawpaw
2 teaspoons honey
2 teaspoons desiccated coconut
6 fresh mint leaves
600 mL orange juice *or* milk

Blend all ingredients and serve in very tall glasses, with a slice of kiwi fruit on the side of the glass. Decorate with a cocktail umbrella or fancy straw.
Serves 4

PASSIONA PUNCH

1½ cups water
1½ cups sugar
1½ teaspoons tartaric acid
pulp 48 passionfruit

Boil water, sugar and tartaric acid until sugar dissolves. While still boiling add passionfruit, beating with a fork for 3 minutes to extract all the juice. Pour into bowl, mix well and bottle.
    To serve, add a small quantity to a glass of water or soda water. If well corked it will keep for some time.
Makes 2½ cups

ICE CREAM MANGO WHIP

2 mangoes, peeled, seeded and chopped
1 cup milk
2 tablespoons honey
3 drops almond essence
2 cups vanilla *or* strawberry ice cream

Combine first 4 ingredients and process until smooth. Add ice cream and process for 10 seconds. Serve immediately with straws and spoons.
Serves 4–6

EMERALD SMOOTHIE

½ avocado, chopped
1 teaspoon honey
1¼ cups milk
2 scoops natural vanilla ice cream
cinnamon, to garnish

Blend all ingredients in blender and serve sprinkled with cinnamon.
Serves 2

MIXED FRUIT CUP

1 pawpaw, peeled and seeded
2 bananas, sliced
1 litre water
1 cup sugar
1 cup orange juice
½ cup lemon juice
pulp 12 passionfruit
2 x 750mL bottles soda water
ice cubes
GARNISH
10 strawberries, sliced
1 orange, thinly sliced
mint leaves

Puree pawpaw and bananas in food processor or blender. Boil water and sugar, stirring for 8–10 minutes until sugar dissolves and thin syrup is formed. Immediately pour onto orange and lemon juices. Add pureed fruit and passionfruit. Chill until needed.
    To serve, add soda water and ice cubes and garnish with strawberries, orange slices and mint leaves.
Makes 3 litres

CHILLED FRUIT PUNCH

1.5 litres cold tea
¾ cup lemon juice
2 cups fresh orange juice
1 litre pineapple juice
1 cup sugar
2.5 litres dry ginger ale
ice cubes
lemon slices
strawberries, hulled
mint leaves, bruised

Combine tea, juices, sugar and chill. Add ginger ale, ice cubes, lemon slices, strawberries and mint leaves.
Makes 30 glasses

Clockwise from top: Party Punch; Ice Cream Mango Whip; Emerald Smoothie

Alcoholic Drinks

CITRUS CHAMPAGNE PUNCH

1 cup sugar
1¼ cups water
grated rind and juice 1 orange *and*
1 lemon
1½ cups grapefruit juice
1½ cups pineapple juice
1.5 litres dry ginger ale
750 mL bottle champagne
ice cubes
orange *and* lemon slices

Dissolve sugar and water in saucepan over medium heat. Add grated rind of orange and lemon and allow to cool. Combine fruit juices and syrup and chill. Before serving, add chilled ginger ale, champagne, ice cubes and fruit slices.
Makes 20 glasses

ZESTY BLOODY MARY

2¼ cups tomato juice
1¼ cups vodka
1½ teaspoons Worcestershire sauce
½ teaspoon chilli sauce
¾ teaspoon celery salt
¼ teaspoon garlic powder
juice 3 limes *or* lemons
ice cubes

Mix all ingredients together, then pour over ice cubes into tall glasses.
Makes 3½ cups

STRAWBERRY DAIQUIRI

8 ice cubes
1 punnet strawberries, hulled
2 tablespoons caster sugar
6 jiggers white rum
juice 2 limes *or* 1 lemon

Crush ice and place in well-chilled glasses. Blend all remaining ingredients and pour over crushed ice. Serve immediately.
Serves 4–6

Left to right: Mixed Fruit Cup; Citrus Champagne Punch; Chilled Fruit Punch

Left to right: Zesty Bloody Mary and Mango and Coconut Delight

JAMAICAN FLOAT

1½ tablespoons fresh orange juice
1½ tablespoons fresh lemon juice
2 teaspoons Orgeate or Maraschino
3 teaspoons brandy
1½ tablespoons light rum
3 ice cubes
   TO SERVE:
2 ice cubes
3 teaspoons rum Negrita
dash grenadine
2 ice cubes

Blend first 6 ingredients, increasing quantity as required. Half-fill a tall chilled glass.

To serve, blend remaining 4 ingredients, float on top of prepared drink and serve garnished with a thin slice of orange.
Serves 1

ALOHA PUNCH

⅓ cup sugar
⅓ cup water
8 whole cloves
1 stick cinnamon
3 cups pineapple juice
3 cups orange juice
⅓ cup lemon juice
2 tablespoons rum
1 litre bottle ginger ale
ice cubes

Combine sugar, water, cloves and cinnamon stick and simmer for 5 minutes. Allow to cool then strain into fruit juices. Chill thoroughly. To serve, mix with rum, ginger ale and ice cubes.
Makes 2.5 litres

SHERRIED TOMATO JUICE

¾ cup tomato juice
salt and pepper, to taste
dash Tabasco sauce
1 teaspoon dry sherry
Worcestershire sauce
lemon wedges, to garnish

Chill the tomato juice then season to taste with the salt, pepper and Tabasco sauce. Just before serving, stir in the sherry and a few drops of Worcestershire sauce to taste. Garnish with a thin wedge of lemon.
Makes 1 cup

TIPSY TOMATO COCKTAIL

3½ cups tomato juice
½ cup claret
½ cup lemon juice
salt and pepper, to taste
pinch paprika
1 teaspoon tomato paste
1 cup cream, whipped

Mix the tomato juice with the claret and lemon juice, then season to taste with salt, pepper and paprika.
  Stir the tomato paste into the cream. Serve the drink chilled and topped with the tomato cream. Garnish with a sprinkling of paprika.
Makes 6 cups

HERBED TOMATO JUICE

1.5 kg tomatoes
½ cup water
1 onion, sliced
1 stick celery, sliced
4 sprigs basil _or_ 1 teaspoon dried basil
3 sprigs parsley
½ bay leaf
pinch salt
pinch paprika
dash Worcestershire sauce
1 teaspoon sherry
lemon juice

Put the tomatoes into a pan with the water, onion, celery and herbs. Simmer until the tomatoes have broken up. Strain, then season to taste with salt, paprika, Worcestershire sauce, sherry and a dash of lemon juice. Pour into a glass and chill before serving.
Makes approximately 4 cups

MINTED TOMATO JUICE

2 cups tomato juice
rind and juice ½ lemon
1 teaspoon vinegar
1 teaspoon Worcestershire sauce
dash Angostura Bitters
1 teaspoon finely chopped mint
salt, pepper and nutmeg, to taste

Combine all the ingredients together and chill thoroughly. Remove the lemon rind before serving.
Makes 2 cups

HAWAIIAN TOMATO DRINK

1½ cups tomato juice
½ cup unsweetened pineapple juice
2 teaspoons Worcestershire sauce
1 teaspoon lemon juice
1 teaspoon rum
pinch salt
pinch cayenne pepper
mint leaves, to garnish

Combine the tomato and pineapple juices with the sauce, lemon juice and rum, then season to taste with the salt and cayenne pepper. Chill thoroughly and serve garnished with mint leaves.
Makes 2 cups

YOGHURT TOMATO MIX

250 g tomatoes, cored, peeled and chopped
200 g carton yoghurt
¼ teaspoon Worcestershire sauce
¼ teaspoon lemon juice
dash Angostura Bitters
paprika
mint leaves, for garnish

Puree the tomatoes in a food processor or blender. Mix the yoghurt, Worcestershire sauce, lemon juice and bitters, then season with a dash of paprika. Chill thoroughly and serve garnished with the mint leaves.
Makes approximately 2 cups

A selection of tomato-based drinks

For Your Information

Glossary of Terms

AUSTRALIA	UK	USA
Equipment and terms		
can	tin	can
crushed	minced	pressed
frying pan	frying pan	skillet
grill	grill	broil
greaseproof paper	greaseproof paper	waxproof paper
lamington tin	oven tray, 4 cm deep	oven tray, 1½ in deep
paper cases	paper baking cases	
paper towel	kitchen paper	white paper towel
patty tin	patty tin	muffin pan
plastic wrap	cling film	plastic wrap
punnet	punnet	basket for 250 g fruit
sandwich tin	sandwich tin	layer cake pan
seeded	stoned	pitted
spring-form cake tin	loose bottomed cake tin	
Swiss roll tin	Swiss roll tin	jelly roll pan
Ingredients		
bacon rasher	bacon rasher	bacon slice
beetroot	beetroot	beets
bicarbonate of soda	bicarbonate of soda	baking soda
black olive	black olive	ripe olive
capsicum	pepper	sweet pepper
caster sugar	caster sugar	granulated table sugar
cornflour	cornflour	cornstarch
cream	single cream	light or coffee cream
crystallised fruit	crystallised fruit	candied fruit
desiccated coconut	desiccated coconut	shredded coconut
eggplant	aubergine	eggplant
essence	essence	extract
five spice	Chinese spice combination of cinnamon, cloves, fennel, star anise and Szechuan pepper	
flour	plain flour	all-purpose flour
glace cherry	glace cherry	candied cherry
green cabbage	white or roundhead cabbage	
hundreds and thousands	hundreds and thousands	non pareils
icing sugar	icing sugar	confectioners' sugar
pawpaw	pawpaw	papaya or papaw
pickled pork	gammon	
prawn	prawn or shrimp	shrimp
rock melon	ogen melon	cantaloupe
self-raising flour	self-raising flour	all-purpose flour with baking powder, 1 cup: 2 teaspoons
shallot	spring onion	scallion
snow pea	mangetout, sugar pea	snow pea
stock cube	stock cube	bouillon cube
sultanas	sultanas	seedless white or golden raisins
tasty cheese	mature Cheddar	
thickened cream	double cream	heavy or whipping cream
tomato puree	tomato puree	tomato paste
tomato sauce	tomato sauce	tomato ketchup
unsalted butter	unsalted butter	sweet butter
wholemeal flour	wholemeal flour	wholewheat flour
yoghurt	natural yoghurt	unflavoured yoghurt
zucchini	courgette	zucchini

If you need to substitute

Fresh fruit: replace with canned or tinned fruit.
Fresh herbs: replace with a quarter of the recommended quantity of dried herbs.
Mulberries: replace with blackcurrants.
Pecans: replace with walnuts.
Rock melons: replace with honeydew melons.
Snapper: replace with any firm white fish such as haddock, cod or whiting.

Oven Temperatures

	Celsius	Fahrenheit
Very slow	120	250
Slow	140–150	275–300
Moderately slow	160	325
Moderate	180	350
Moderately hot	190	375
Hot	200	400
	220	425
	230	450
Very hot	250–260	475–500

Measurements

Standard Metric Measures

1 cup	=	250 mL
1 tablespoon	=	20 mL
1 teaspoon	=	5 mL

All spoon measurements are level

Cup Measures

1 x 250 mL cup =	Grams	Ounces
breadcrumbs, dry	125	4½
soft	60	2
butter	250	8¾
cheese, grated		
cheddar	125	4½
coconut, desiccated	95	3¼
flour, cornflour	130	4¾
plain or self-raising	125	4½
wholemeal	135	4¾
fruit, mixed dried	160	5¾
honey	360	12¾
sugar, caster	225	7¾
crystalline	250	8¾
icing	175	6¾
moist brown	170	6
nuts	125	4

Index

Acknowledgements

The publisher would like to thank the following for providing cutlery, glassware and tableware for the photography of this book.
The Bay Tree for tableware (pages 22, 24, 34, 36, 37, 64, 69, 70, 71)
Dansab for tableware (pages 22, 33, 48, 51, 55, 64, 66, 69, 89)
Decor Gifts for tableware (pages 30, 86, 87, 91)
Glass Artist for glassware (page 28)
Grace Brothers for tableware (pages 5, 13, 15, 18, 24, 35, 62, 63, 78, 79, 90, 91)
Jeorg Jenson for cutlery (pages 46, 69, 78, 79)
Lifestyle Imports for tableware (pages 18, 19, 22, 35)
Made Where for tableware (pages 20, 35, 46, 66, 72, 73, 75)
Mosman Design Store for glassware (page 90)
Wedgewood for tableware (pages 24, 38, 76, 77, 82, 83, 84, 85)